BELGIUM

1939–1940

BELGIUM

*The Official Account of
what happened
1939-1940*

Published for

THE BELGIAN MINISTRY OF FOREIGN AFFAIRS

by

EVANS BROTHERS LIMITED, LONDON

CONTENTS 17153

CHAPTER   PAGE

INTRODUCTION ix

I. THE INTERNATIONAL SITUATION OF BELGIUM BEFORE THE CONFLICT 1

II. BELGIUM AND THE EUROPEAN CONFLICT . . . 7

III. THE GERMAN AGGRESSION 26

IV. HOW THE BELGIAN ARMY DEFENDED THE TERRITORY 32

APPENDICES

1. Speech by the King to the Council of Ministers on October 14th, 1936 53

2. Franco-British Declaration of April 24th, 1937 . . 56

3. Speech in the Chamber of Representatives by M. Spaak, Minister for Foreign Affairs, on April 29th, 1937 . 57

4. German Declaration of October 13th, 1937 . . 67

5. Declaration made by King Leopold on behalf of the Heads of the States of the Oslo Group, August 23rd, 1939 68

6. Declaration made by the Ambassador of Germany on August 26th, 1939 69

7. Declarations made by the Ambassadors of Great Britain and France on August 27th and 28th, 1939 . 70

8. Declaration of Neutrality, September 3rd, 1939. 72

9. The King's Order of the Day to the Army, September 4th, 1939 77

10. Speech by the King, Broadcast to the United States on October 27th, 1939 77

11. Telegram from Queen Wilhelmina and King Leopold to the Heads of the States of Germany, France, and Great Britain, dated November 7th, 1939 . . 79

APPENDICES (*continued*)

12. Speech in the Chamber of Representatives by M. Spaak, Minister for Foreign Affairs, on December 19th, 1939 80

13. Secret Instruction to the Commander of the Second Luftflotte found in a German Aeroplane on January 10th, 1940 85

14. Speech in the Senate by M. Spaak, Minister for Foreign Affairs, on April 16th, 1940 91

15. Note by the Ministry of National Defence, dated March 28th, 1940, on the Defensive Works carried out since the Beginning of the Conflict 96

16. Measures taken by Belgium to strengthen the National Defence System 97

17. Text of the Protest drawn up by the Belgian Government against the German Aggression of May 10th, 1940 100

18. Proclamation by King Leopold, May 10th, 1940 . 102

19. German Leaflets dropped in the Belgian Lines . . 102

20. King Leopold's Order of the Day, May 25th, 1940 . 104

21. Statement by Lieut.-Colonel Robert Duncan Brown, United States Military Attaché to Belgium and Luxemburg 104

22. The Belgian Campaign: Sir Roger Keyes *v. Daily Mirror*. (High Court of Justice, June 13th, 1941) . 106

LIST OF ILLUSTRATIONS

PAGE

COPY OF A DECLARATION MADE BY THE FRENCH AMBASSA-
DOR, AUGUST 28TH, 1939 71

FACING PAGES

COPY OF SECRET INSTRUCTIONS OF THE GERMAN COMMAND 88, 89

PAGE

COPY OF GERMAN LEAFLETS DROPPED IN THE BELGIAN LINES 103

THE KING'S ORDER OF THE DAY TO THE ARMY, MAY 25TH,
1940 105

LIST OF MAPS

FACING PAGE

MAP 1: THE POSITION ON MAY 10TH, 1940 . . . 32

MAP 2: THE GERMAN DESCENT ON THE LINE EBEN–
EMAEL–BRIEGDEN, MAY 10TH, 1940 . . . 34

MAP 3: THE POSITION ON MAY 13TH, 1940 . . . 38

MAP 4: THE THREAT TO ABBEVILLE, MAY 20TH, 1940 . 42

MAP 5: THE LAST STAND, MAY 26TH–27TH, 1940 . 48

INTRODUCTION

THIS is no time to embark on a complete history of the war in Belgium—too many essential facts are still missing.

The German offensive of May 1940 was so dramatic and had such devastating results that it made a very deep impression on public opinion. People were badly shaken by such unexpected events; they were bewildered, and found it difficult to understand what had happened. Under the emotional strain of those critical hours, feeling was so intense that the facts were distorted and twisted. The popular imagination seized on the kind of explanation that always flourishes in time of trouble: the disaster was said to be due to treason or, to use the current expression, to the work of a Fifth Column which was said to be assuming alarming proportions. Amongst thinking people some deemed it wiser to suspend judgment.

A year has now elapsed. Many new facts have gradually come to light and their accuracy has been tested. We are also a little farther away and are able to judge them in their true perspective.

In these circumstances, we have thought fit to bring together such of the principal documents as we have been able to obtain. They are arranged in chronological order, and are preceded by a commentary putting them in their proper setting and showing the connexion between them. The comments also describe the mission assigned to Belgium, in agreement with the neighbouring Powers, in the arrangements for guaranteeing the security of Western Europe, and what she did to fulfil it. With the help of these documents, the reader should be able to form his own judgment.

The series comes to an end with the surrender which brought the campaign of the Belgian Army to a close on May 28th. A second work on similar lines will deal with the steps taken by Belgium—with the co-operation of the British Government and the other Governments engaged in the common fight—to free her national territory.

July, 1941.

I

THE INTERNATIONAL SITUATION OF BELGIUM BEFORE THE CONFLICT

WHEN Belgium's independence was guaranteed under the Treaties of 1839, a regime of perpetual neutrality was imposed on her. In 1918, the British and French Governments recognized that the changed situation in Europe made the restoration of this regime out of the question. For four years the Belgian Army fought side by side with the British and French Armies to free Belgium's national territory. After the Armistice, she shared the occupation of the left bank of the Rhine with them. In 1920, the Belgian and French General Staffs reached an agreement fixing the technical details of military co-operation between Belgium and France in the event of a fresh unprovoked aggression by Germany. At that time Germany was far from having reduced her armaments to the limits laid down in the Treaty of Versailles. At the same time Belgium was anxious to conclude with Great Britain an arrangement providing for her security. But she was unable to overcome the objections raised by the British Government. A proposal was, however, made in 1922. It provided that should Germany make a direct unprovoked attack on Belgium, Great Britain would immediately come to her assistance with all her naval, military, and air forces, on the understanding that in such a contingency Belgium would defend her own frontiers with all her military, naval, and air forces. This proposal was turned down by the British Government because the condition laid down by Great Britain—a similar agreement with France—could not be fulfilled.

Belgium hoped to obtain new guarantees through the League of Nations. She played an active part in drawing up the Covenant. She was a Member of the Council without a break until 1926. In 1920, her Minister for Foreign Affairs was President of the Assembly. On many occasions, particularly over the Corfu incident, she did not hesitate to insist on the application of the Covenant to Great Powers with whom she was on friendly terms. In 1936, despite her ties with Italy, her first Delegate declared that Belgium would carry out all her obligations with regard to the application of sanctions. She assisted actively in the League's attempts to secure the limitation and gradual reduction of armaments, and several of her delegates played an important part in this field.

In 1925, Belgium, together with Great Britain, France, Germany, and Italy, signed the Locarno Agreements. She assumed a rôle in the organization of Western Europe which was subsequently to prove out of all proportion to the force at the disposal of a small State. That is to say, she undertook to assist Germany in the event of a French aggression or France in the event of a German aggression. But the risk seemed quite theoretical at that time. Europe appeared to be entering upon a period of pacification, concord, and international co-operation.

Before long, however, matters took a very different turn and disillusionment set in. The economic depression of 1930 had a shattering effect on Europe. Unemployment and poverty increased the feeling of discontent that was already beginning to find expression among the unsatisfied nations, and their nationalism became increasingly revolutionary and aggressive in character. The coming into power of the Hitler regime precipitated matters. It is only necessary, by way of a reminder, to mention a few of the more outstanding events.

After Hitler became Chancellor of the Reich on January 30th, 1933, Germany withdrew ostentatiously from the League of Nations and the Disarmament Conference. This happened on October 14th. On June 14th, 1934, Hitler and Mussolini had their first meeting at Venice; on March 16th, 1935, Germany repudiated the military, naval, and air clauses of the Treaty of Versailles, and announced that conscription would be introduced. This followed upon the announcement, a few days earlier, of the formation of a military air force; on October 2nd of the same year, Italy invaded Ethiopia in flagrant violation of the provisions of the Covenant of the League of Nations. On March 7th, 1936, German troops reoccupied the left bank of the Rhine and the Treaty of Locarno was repudiated; on July 4th, the League of Nations admitted that sanctions had failed and discontinued them. On July 17th, civil war broke out in Spain.

These events, which followed upon one another with increasing rapidity and were of increasing gravity, were a warning to Belgium of new threats to the peace of Europe and consequently to her own security. By reducing her own armaments, Great Britain had allowed Germany to steal a march on her which she was unable to overtake; France was weakened by a long financial, industrial, and social crisis. The international order created after the World War was no longer secure.

In 1930, Belgium took certain measures to strengthen the defences of the country. Parliament passed a plan for restoring and modernizing the Belgian fortifications. In particular, the positions of Liège and Namur were reinforced. New lines of defence were established along the canal from Maastricht to Bois-le-Duc, the canal joining the Meuse and Escaut and the Albert Canal.

The protection of the eastern frontier, based mainly on the destruction of a number of roads, was entrusted to new formations (frontier cyclist units, " Chasseurs Ardennais ").

In the spring of 1935, these measures were almost complete, but even then they were no longer adequate. A conflagration might break out suddenly. There was not sufficient protection against such a risk. In order that the safety of the country might at all times be ensured, the period of military service had to be prolonged, and provision was made for this in a new Bill, but it was opposed by a large section of the public. This was due, to a considerable extent, to suspicion of Belgium's international engagements:

it was feared that they would involve her in conflicts far from home. The Coalition Government, consisting of Catholics, Socialists, and Liberals, then in power, had so far been unable to break down this prejudice. It was then that the King, conscious of his constitutional duties, made a new attempt to convince his Ministers of the need for improving the defences of the country, while at the same time allaying the anxiety of those who feared the risks involved by Belgium's international obligations. That is the significance of the statement he made at the meeting of the Council convened at the Palace on October 14th, 1936 (Appendix 1). His speech made a great impression on the members of the Government; it was thought likely to remove the objections of the opponents of the Bill, and the King was asked whether it might be made public. The precise significance of the speech was not understood abroad; it was taken as a new departure in Belgian policy. The only passage to attract attention was that relating to the international situation of Belgium. At first sight, it was not realized that, from the Government's point of view, the object of the speech and the reason why it was published was to gain the support of the Belgian public for the proposal to strengthen the national defences.

The British and French Governments, who had been better informed, had no doubt as to the position. They recognized that in the existing state of affairs in Europe Belgium's attitude was justified. They readily admitted that any aggression of which she was the victim would constitute a direct threat to the neighbouring Powers; that by protecting access to her territory, Belgium was making the most effective contribution towards the security of the surrounding States; that in this way she was doing her utmost to fulfil her function in this part of Europe which was so often exposed to the ravages of war.

It was in these circumstances that the Franco-British Declaration of April 24th, 1937, was made (Appendix 2).

The British and French Governments took note of Belgium's determination, expressed publicly and on more than one occasion, to defend her frontiers with all her forces against any aggression or invasion, and to prevent Belgian territory from being used, for purposes of aggression against another State, as a passage or as a base of operations by land, by sea, or in the air. They therefore released Belgium from her undertakings to render assistance under the Locarno Treaty, while maintaining their own undertakings to render assistance to Belgium under the Treaty.

The British and French Governments also took note of the renewed assurances of the Belgian Government " of the fidelity of Belgium to the Covenant of the League of Nations and to the obligations which it involves for Members of the League." Belgian policy was always based on that principle, but experience had shown that the coercive measures provided for in Article 16 of the Covenant were inoperative. In practice, as was clear at the time of the Sino-Japanese dispute in 1931, they were regarded as optional. This was explicitly recognized by most of the Members of the League of Nations at the 1938 Assembly, and their application was not even demanded when Germany committed acts of aggression in 1939. It may be remarked here that the Treaty of Locarno could not have been invoked had it remained in force. It did not guarantee Poland, but only the *status quo* on the Rhineland frontiers. Belgium was only to assist France in the event of an unprovoked act of aggression by Germany, and to assist Germany in the event of an unprovoked act of aggression by France. Neither of these two contingencies occurred. The decision of the British and French Governments to release Belgium from her obligation was not therefore in any way to change her position with regard to the events which marked the opening of the European conflict.

Nevertheless, the negotiations undertaken after the repudiation of the Treaty of Locarno by Germany with a view to replacing the Treaty by a new general Act continued. England had not at that time lost all hope of bringing them to a successful conclusion. No doubt she had begun to rearm. But in November 1936, the Prime Minister, Mr.

Baldwin, admitted that there had been some delay, and in the spring of 1937 his successor, Mr. Chamberlain, showed his determination to combine the strengthening of defence measures with " a substantial effort to remove the causes which are delaying the return of confidence in Europe." This attempt was to continue until 1939, and it was only abandoned a very few months before the beginning of the war.

That, at any rate, was the atmosphere in Europe in 1937. In January, Chancellor Hitler declared that he was prepared at any moment to recognize the inviolability of Belgian territory. Following up this intention he made a declaration to the Belgian Government on October 13th, the most important passages of which repeat the words of the Franco-British Declaration of April 24th (Appendix 4).

The two declarations sanctioned what the Belgian Government has described as a " policy of independence." It used this expression in order to draw a distinction between that policy and the neutrality of Belgium, as laid down contractually before the German aggression in 1914; it intended at the same time to indicate that it reserved full liberty to act at any time in the interests of the country. If, bearing in mind the unstable situation in Europe, it restricted Belgium's international undertakings, that was first from motives of honesty: it did not want to undertake obligations which were regarded as excessive by a large section of the public and which it was not sure of being able to fulfil. Secondly, it was with the intention of concentrating the national forces. If they were all to be mobilized, it was necessary that the country should concentrate on one urgent and indisputable duty, and one only—national defence. It was essential that immediately an act of aggression was committed, the whole nation, fully aware that it was blameless, should rise up as one man, just as it did in August 1914 (Appendix 3).[1]

[1] Mr. Winston Churchill defended a similar policy in Parliament on November 23rd, 1932, when he said: " Their duty is not only to try, within the restricted limits which, I fear, are all that is open to them, to prevent war, but to make sure that we ourselves are not involved in one, and, above all, to make sure that, if war should break out among other Powers, our country and the King's Dominions can be effectively defended, and will be able to preserve, if they desire to do so, that strong and unassailable neutrality from

II

BELGIUM AND THE EUROPEAN CONFLICT

IN the spring of 1939, when Germany suddenly invaded Czechoslovak territory, no shadow of doubt remained: Europe was moving rapidly towards a general conflict. This was a distressing prospect for all peace-loving nations. Belgium, though she felt powerless before the coming storm, continued to the end to do everything in her power to ward it off.

She had not forgotten the Great War and four years of enemy occupation. She realized that the totalitarian countries, with their worship of force, would display unparalleled brutality in a new war. She was also aware that they had forged a formidable weapon to ensure superiority on land and in the air, and above all, that their Air Force was far bigger than the Air Forces of the great Democracies.

Belgium reflected upon the ordeal which faced Europe and a great part of mankind; she also reflected upon the risks to which she was herself exposed. Her policy had undoubtedly been a prudent one, and at the same time she had made a great military effort. But experience had taught her that, in spite of declarations and solemn undertakings, she would be in grave danger, in the event of a European conflict, of being used once again as the battlefield of the Great Powers.

Her anxiety was shared by the small States on the North Sea and the Baltic, which had for several years been in the

which we must never be drawn except by the heart and conscience of the nation."

In a speech in Parliament on March 8th, 1934, he reverted to the same idea: " . . . But, putting the preservation of peace in the first place, what is the next great object that we must have in view ? It is to secure our national freedom of choice to remain outside a European war, if one should break out. That I put as the more direct and more practical issue, subordinate to, but not less important than, the preservation of peace."

2

habit, under the name of the Oslo Group, of exchanging views from time to time about questions of mutual interest connected with the League of Nations. These consultations took place in a spirit of great cordiality and mutual confidence, and had, of course, nothing to do with political or military obligations. Thus, in July 1938, when the international situation already looked black on account of events in Czechoslovakia, the Foreign Ministers of the Oslo States met at Copenhagen, and after their exchange of views declared themselves " prepared, for their part, to collaborate in any international attempt at conciliation in a spirit of impartiality and independence towards the various groups of Powers."

In August 1939, war seemed to be imminent. The Governments of these small States accepted a suggestion put forward by Belgium and agreed to make a last effort to save peace. When negotiations between the Great Powers seemed to be broken off for good and all, an appeal on humanitarian grounds might possibly enable them to set aside motives of prestige and reopen conversations. The Foreign Ministers were convened urgently to Brussels on August 23rd, where they adopted a declaration. King Leopold, speaking on behalf of the heads of the Oslo States, read this declaration to the whole world on the same day at the Brussels Palace (Appendix 5). It was a heartrending appeal to public opinion to pull itself together and not to succumb to the idea that a catastrophe was inevitable. But although the appeal called for a pacific settlement, there was no ambiguity, no question of resignation in the face of violence and accomplished facts. " Let there be no mistake!" said the King. " The peace that we want is peace with respect for the rights of all nations. A durable peace cannot be based on force. It can only be based on a moral order."

The Pope and many Governments associated themselves with the appeal. The British and French Governments fully sympathized, and pointed out that they had always urged the settlement by pacific methods of all international disputes. Germany and Italy made no comment.

A few days later, on August 26th, the German Ambassador at his own request was received by the King in the presence of the Prime Minister.   He declared of his own accord that the Government of the Reich was firmly determined to comply with the terms of the German Declaration of October 13th, 1937, according to which the Reich would in no circumstances impair the inviolability and integrity of Belgium, but would at all times respect Belgian territory (Appendix 6).

On the following days, the Ambassadors of Great Britain and France also gave an assurance, on behalf of their Governments, that should the efforts of these Governments to maintain peace fail, and should Belgium, in such a contingency, adopt an attitude of neutrality, they were resolved, in accordance with their traditional policy, fully to respect Belgium's neutrality (Appendix 7).

On August 28th, the situation became even more critical. Queen Wilhelmina and King Leopold, being anxious to the last to leave nothing undone, however slight, to avert the danger, made an offer of their good offices to Great Britain, France, Poland, Germany, and Italy.   The representatives of these countries were called upon one by one by M. Pierlot in Brussels and simultaneously by M. van Kleffens at The Hague.[1]

But nothing could be done to stem the tide of events.

On September 1st, the German Army entered Poland. Germany refused to withdraw her troops, and Great Britain and France therefore considered themselves to be in a state of war with her on September 3rd.

The dreaded disaster had occurred.

From that time Belgium's duty was plain.   It had been clearly laid down in 1936; it was not discussed and there was no ambiguity about it.   Great Britain and France on the one hand and Germany on the other had taken note of it in 1937, solemnly indicating their approval.   Furthermore, they had confirmed it several days earlier in their statements

[1] The offer was renewed on November 7th in circumstances which will be described later on.

of August 26th, 27th, 28th, 1939. " Once again I arrived at the reassuring conviction," said the Foreign Minister in the Chamber on April 16th, 1940, " that our foreign policy had been . . . perfectly correct. Few countries can have defined their objectives so clearly; confined themselves to promises they could be sure of keeping; enlightened their neighbours as to their intentions. There was not—there is not —any change, any element of surprise. Whatever happens, nobody can say Belgium deceived them " (Appendix 14).

Now that the Great Powers of the West were at war with one another, Belgium had to follow the policy she had adopted.

Politically, she was in much the same position as in 1914. She realized that, as in 1914, it was in her highest interest faithfully and loyally to fulfil her international obligations. She was under no obligation to take part in the war. The Rhine Pact did not apply, and in any case it did not bind her. The League of Nations was not asked to take action, and if it had been, its recommendations would have been optional.

On the other hand, the position taken note of in the Declarations of Great Britain, France, and Germany in 1937 implied that in such a conflict Belgium would be neutral. She had therefore to fulfil the obligations imposed on neutral States under international law. On September 3rd, the *Moniteur* published the Belgian Declaration of Neutrality (Appendix 8).

In the economic sphere, difficult questions immediately arose, because the belligerents took opposing views. The Belgian Government based all its negotiations with them on two principles. First, it endeavoured to safeguard Belgian interests autonomously by prohibiting or regulating the export of such foodstuffs and essential raw materials as were not produced in sufficient quantities to meet the needs of the country. The second principle was based on Article 9 of the Hague Convention, which prohibited neutral States from imposing any prohibition or restriction on a belligerent State which it did not similarly impose on other belligerent States.

These two principles were hardly open to question. They

did, of course, involve a heavy reduction in Belgian exports to Germany; but there was no legal ground for Germany's protests. Great Britain and France recognized that they provided all the guarantees they could reasonably expect. Belgium's duty was most obvious in the military sphere. Here, it is sufficient to refer to the terms of the Declarations of 1937, when Germany, as well as Great Britain and France, took note of the Belgian Government's determination (a) to defend the frontiers of Belgium with all its forces against any aggression or invasion, and to prevent Belgian territory from being used, for purposes of aggression against any other State, as a passage or as a base of operations by land, by sea, or in the air; (b) to organize the defence of Belgium in an efficient manner for this purpose.

Since 1912 Belgium had had a system of compulsory general service. In peace-time she had six infantry divisions and two cavalry divisions, forming three army corps and one cavalry corps. From 1934 there were also frontier guard units and the " Chasseurs Ardennais." In war-time Belgium could, by means of general mobilization, raise an army of twenty infantry divisions, one cavalry corps and troops for the fortifications—about 650,000 men in all.

In 1930, as we have already seen, she restored and improved her fortifications; in 1935 she tried to provide greater protection by extending the period of service, and this was increased to seventeen months under a law passed at the beginning of 1937; at the same time, she maintained her annual contingent in spite of the years when the birth-rate was low; she improved and added to her material, mechanized the whole of the cavalry, and extended and developed the training of units on active service and in the reserve.

When the crisis occurred in September 1938, she called up several classes and put twelve infantry divisions on a war-time footing. Partial mobilization was costly, but it was a useful experiment and enabled improvements to be made. A more flexible system was introduced by which mobilization was divided into five successive stages, A to E.

As a frontier country at the outposts of Germany and

France, Belgium had to be on her guard, during an international crisis, immediately the neighbouring Powers took military measures, so as to avoid being taken by surprise. As in the past, this rule was scrupulously observed.

As from August 24th and 25th, Army leave was cancelled and soldiers on leave were recalled. On the 25th was decided Stage A of mobilization. This was the first of the provisions for putting our military machine on a war-time footing. On the 26th a Royal Decree declared that the country was in a state of mobilization. Its object was to bring about the entry into force of several legislative and administrative measures provided for in the event of an international crisis. The Decree was therefore not an order for general mobilization. On the contrary, it explained that mobilization of the Army would be spread over several stages on the orders of the Minister of National Defence. On August 28th, mobilization passed to Stage B; this involved the supervision and guarding of the frontiers, aerial protection and observation. The garrisons of fortified positions were reinforced. At the same time, all private and foreign aircraft were prohibited from flying over Belgian territory and territorial waters, with the exception of aircraft of regular lines and aircraft holding an authorization from the Ministry of Communications.

On the opening of hostilities in Poland, the Minister of National Defence ordered Stage C of mobilization, which involved the calling up of units of the first reserve. This was completed by September 3rd.

On September 4th, the King issued an Order of the Day under Article 68 of the Constitution, announcing that he had taken command of the Army (Appendix 9). On the 10th, a number of second reserve units were recalled for a period of training.

During September, the German offensive was aimed at Poland; the western front remained calm. France did not have sufficient effectives, or material, or aeroplanes to engage successfully in offensive operations. By the middle of September, mobilization was proceeding systematically, and about fifty divisions had been called up. England had sent three divisions to the Continent.

At that time, Poland had already virtually succumbed to the attacks of armoured divisions and a formidable air force. The campaign in the east was at an end, and in a speech in the Reichstag on October 6th, Chancellor Hitler described the results achieved. In the favourable circumstances produced by his military successes, he seemed disposed to enter into peace negotiations. However, the German armies were brought back from the eastern front and the whole of the forces were placed on the western frontier. Over fifty divisions were concentrated on the left bank of the Rhine on the frontiers of southern Holland and Belgium. From that moment hardly a week passed without the Belgian military authorities receiving information of steady reinforcements of both men and materials in this area : new divisions, the number facing the Dutch and Belgian frontiers increasing to nearly seventy; large quantities of material for bridge-building for crossing watercourses, munition dumps, aerodromes, etc. The Belgian Army Command was therefore compelled progressively to increase its precautionary measures, and to carry on with the mobilization of the Army, so that it was soon almost up to a wartime footing.

On several occasions the Belgian military authorities received information which led them to fear an immediate act of aggression. The effect of these warnings was to speed up the mobilization of the Belgian forces and to stimulate arrangements for putting the country in a complete state of defence.

The first "alert" occurred at the end of October. Holland appeared specially threatened. According to information reaching the Netherlands authorities, a surprise German attack was to be launched at dawn on Sunday, November 12th. Alarming signs were brought simultaneously to the notice of the Belgian Government.

The Minister for Foreign Affairs of the Netherlands has

described how he decided, in the circumstances, to suggest
to Queen Wilhelmina that she should renew the offer of
good offices previously made on August 28th in conjunction
with King Leopold.[1] This suggestion was made in Brussels
on Monday, November 6th. So that no time should be lost,
the King left for The Hague the same evening, accompanied
by the Minister for Foreign Affairs and his Military Adviser.
The draft was completed on the following morning and was
sent in the afternoon to the King of England, the President
of the French Republic, and the Chancellor of the German
Reich (Appendix 11). Alarming news about Germany's
military intentions continued to arrive during the next few
days, and it appeared to confirm that an attack was imminent.
Then, all of a sudden, the plans for aggression seemed to
have been abandoned. Was this really the case, or was it
only a blind ? Even now it is impossible to be sure. However, the information as a whole was sufficient to justify
most elaborate precautions.

During the first fortnight of January, there was another
grave warning, and all forms of national defence were
pushed forward as quickly as possible.

A German courier plane made a forced landing at
Mechelen-sur-Meuse in Belgian territory on January 10th.
The two officers on board said that they had lost their way
in the fog above the Ruhr basin and the valley of the Rhine.
One of the two officers had some confidential papers which
he twice tried to burn. He almost succeeded the second
time: he managed to throw them suddenly into a lighted
stove while he was being questioned, but a Belgian officer
rushed forward, put his hand in the stove and pulled them
out of the flames three-parts burned. They consisted of
instructions to the squadron-leader of No. 2 Air Fleet about
the offensive which the German Western Army was to carry
out across Belgium from the Moselle to the North Sea.
The Sixth German Army was specially instructed to destroy
the Belgian Army, launching its main attack in the Maastricht
district; the Seventh Air Force Division, conveyed by air, was

[1] Van Kleffens, *The Rape of the Netherlands*, pp. 85–8.

to land between the Sambre and the Meuse (Appendix 13).

Was the document authentic ?   Was it really an accident that it had fallen into the hands of the Belgian Army ?   A thorough enquiry was made, and the hypothesis of a trick was dismissed.   It was certainly a severe winter, and snow and frost hardly seemed propitious to military operations. But it was clear from the papers that it would be easier for German air-borne troops to land if the ground was hard with frost.   Other disturbing news which came to hand at the same time seemed to confirm this.   It was feared that the German Command, learning that important parts of the plan of operations had fallen into the hands of the Belgian authorities, would carry it through at once, so that there would be no time to counter the attack.

As this plan involved a threat to England, France, the Netherlands, as well as Belgium, their military authorities were immediately informed.

The Army remained at the ready for several days; then, as no important troop movements on the frontier had been reported, it was concluded that the attack had again been postponed.

However, important additions were made to the Belgian defences.   The Army continued to organize its positions.

The Belgian Army was disposed as a covering force on positions along the Albert Canal from Antwerp to Liège and along the Meuse from Liège to Namur.   Advanced units and demolition squads deployed from the German and Netherlands frontier were to hamper the invader and prevent contact on this protective position.   This was a very strong position, and the natural obstacles were supplemented and reinforced by means of a large number of fortifications and fieldworks.   But there were three serious drawbacks:

(1) It was a long way from the French frontier.
(2) It was very extended (over 200 kilometres).
(3) It was semi-elliptical.

Owing to its distance from the French frontier, no Franco-British help could be expected on that line.   Yet by itself the Belgian Army could not engage the German forces on a front of over 200 kilometres without running the risk of being annihilated. Again, being a semi-ellipse with the point at Liège, it was dangerously exposed to flank attacks, particularly in the north, where a local break-through would irreparably threaten the whole position.

Quite clearly the Albert-Meuse Canal position could only be a covering position. If the Belgian Army were to offer resistance there, the Franco-British forces and the bulk of the Belgian Army would have time to occupy a position connecting the fortified towns of Antwerp and Namur. This line, which runs through Koningshoyckt–Malines–Louvain–Wavre, is known as the K.W. position, after the places at either end. The construction of the line K.W. was begun in 1939. The experience gained during the construction of the Liège and Namur fortifications and the lessons learnt from the Spanish War were largely taken into account. The K.W. position comprised a large number of works spread over several lines. The front was protected by a continuous anti-tank barrier and by arrangements for flooding, while anti-tank traps were provided well inside the position. There was also an underground telephone system and a road system.

The Belgian line thus embraced the fortified town of Antwerp, the K.W. line, and the fortified town of Namur. On this position—supported at the North Sea by the fortified town of Antwerp and extended south and connected with the Maginot Line by the Meuse cutting—the Belgian Army—with the help of the Franco-British forces, expected on the third day of the war—had decided to engage in the battle which was to stem the invasion.

This defence line had for long been known as one of the most important strategic lines in Western Europe. It was very near the line of the armies of Louis XIV when Belgium was defended against the Coalition forces under Marlborough.

The Belgians are well aware of the price their country has had to pay for the doubtful privilege of being used as a

battlefield by its powerful neighbours.   It was therefore not
without some apprehension that the Belgian Government
contemplated the stabilization of the front on the Antwerp–
Namur line.   Indeed, its choice meant the certain destruction of the chief towns of Belgium—Brussels, Antwerp,
Malines, Louvain, Namur, Lierre, Gembloux.   It also meant
handing over half the national territory to the enemy.

The fortifications were not confined to the K.W. line.
The other positions were constantly improved.   Preparations were made for extensive destructions, particularly of
roads, all along the front and in the Ardennes; all the
bridges and principal routes were mined; obstacles were
placed everywhere.   On the National Railway Company's
system alone 137 kilometres of track, 310 points and cross-
ings, and 339 bridges and tunnels had been destroyed by the
end of the May campaign.

Full advantage was taken of the months gained at the
beginning of the war—fieldworks were under construction,
reserve formations were called up and thoroughly trained.
Belgium had at that time twenty infantry divisions, one
motorized brigade, and a mechanized cavalry corps not only
well-equipped, armed and officered, but trained and familiar
with the ground.   All the higher officers and many of the
reserve officers were veterans of the 1914 war; they had
taken part in the victorious offensive of 1918, and still
remembered the victory over the German armies.   The
troops were proud of their strength, the worth of their
material, the soundness of their positions.

To form a strong army of 600,000, Belgium had to
mobilize 8 per cent. of her total population, or 46 per cent.
of the men between twenty and forty years of age.   It was
a tremendous effort and strain (Appendix 16).

Although the soldiers' pay and the allowances to the
families of those who were called up were relatively small,
mobilization involved financial burdens which were crushing
in comparison with Belgium's resources.   At the beginning
of 1940, the daily expenditure, including extraordinary
expenditure on fortifications, was 21 million francs.   Other

extraordinary expenditure amounted to 3·5 million francs a day; the ordinary budget was 12 thousand million francs per annum; the total estimated to be borne by the State in 1941 amounted to nearly 21 thousand million francs.

Though great sacrifices were made, the national defences were not complete. The Air Force was not up to the same standard as the Army. The reason is simple. Technical progress is so rapid that air material is soon out of date. It has therefore to be written off after a short time, and this entails considerable expense. The Army had British machines, and when the danger became more acute, Belgium tried to obtain more. But British industry had to meet pressing national requirements, and the Belgian Army was only able to obtain a few Hurricanes.

Another factor had to be taken into account. The aerodromes of a frontier country like Belgium are highly exposed, because of their proximity to the German bases. Belgian material, despite the precautions taken, was in danger of being destroyed during a sudden attack. In any event, in such a contingency, Belgium could not expect to defend herself without help. She was counting on the aid of the Powers that had given their guarantee. In the air, this help appeared to be possible at once. Belgium was justified in relying on the French and British Air Forces to defend her skies.

Although Belgian air power was weak, Belgium did her duty, thanks to her fully organized observer corps and to the courage of her pilots, when belligerent aircraft flew over her territory.

In taking steps to safeguard the defences of the country, she followed the dictates of conscience as to her duty to herself and to other States. She was convinced that Belgian interests were the same as the interests of the Powers with whom she sympathized. Parliamentary debates, Government declarations in both France and England, left no doubt that the rearmament of these Powers was not up to the same standard as that of Germany. It was known that the industrial mobilization and material assistance of the United States would not be fully effective for a long time. During that period, Belgium protected the vital areas of England and France. As far as the latter was concerned, a French General remarked in a well-known book that Belgian neutrality, as long as it was respected, " would strengthen France considerably . . . by reducing the length of our front of 250 kilometres which the Belgian Army could not hold alone." [1]

Great prominence had been given in the Belgian Press, during the spring of 1940, to statements made in England according to which it was fortunate that Germany had not launched a full-scale attack on the western front at the beginning of the war. It was said that time had thus been given to France and England to pursue the mobilization of their national resources and bring their war effort to the maximum.

Eminent French publicists have since disclosed that M. Daladier, President of the Council, and General Gamelin, were concerned in the same way about their country.[2]

Belgian public opinion noted with satisfaction the increasing evidence that the requirements of national defence were in keeping with her sympathies, for she did not admit that political neutrality meant she must keep silent. " This voluntary neutrality," said M. Max, Burgomaster of Brussels, at a meeting of the Communal Council on September 17th, 1939, " is fully in keeping with the dignity appropriate to a proud people. It does not prevent either independence of thought, or liberty of conscience, or loyalty to our friends." Public opinion was suspicious of any attempt to check these sentiments. Moreover, the Government, though recommending moderation, affirmed the same principle. " No one," said the Minister for Foreign Affairs in the Chamber on September 19th, " has ever maintained that a neutral Belgian must be an indifferent Belgian. And the history of to-day cannot efface the history of yesterday.

---

[1] General Chauvineau, *Une invasion est-elle encore possible*, p. 193.
[2] Elie J. Bois, *Truth on the Tragedy of France*, pp. 98, 170; André Maurois, *Tragédie en France*, p. 77.

Such truths have often been proclaimed, and not a member of the Government would deny them." The Minister's words were thus in harmony with those of the Burgomaster of Brussels.

The Government, with the approval of public opinion, was careful to see that Belgian independence and national dignity were maintained. The Press severely criticized German acts of aggression as well as violations of international law and of the most elementary laws of humanity. Germany protested in vain at such freedom of opinion. She induced all the neutral States of Europe to prohibit the sale of the books which were most critical of the dangers and evils of Hitler's Reich, such as those of Dr. Rauschning and Otto Strasser. Brussels was approached many times in the same sense, but refused.

The Minister for Foreign Affairs, speaking in Parliament, condemned the Russian aggression in Finland. "The Government," said M. Spaak, on December 19th, "is indignant." In the same spirit of independence, speaking in the Senate on April 16th, he expressed Belgium's sympathy with Norway, which had been suddenly attacked. "We are following Norway's efforts all the more sympathetically," he said, "in that she was always a great lover of peace and was loyally neutral." (Hear, hear. Applause from all benches.) "She was therefore in much the same position as ourselves. Her sentiments were our sentiments " (Appendix 14).

The Minister did not stop there. He warned Belgium of the lesson to be learnt from this bitter experience. "What strikes me most," he said, "in Norway's heroic stand is that love of peace, respect for neutrality, the often-repeated desire to spare one's country the horrors of war do not in any way diminish but rather heighten the fierce determination to defend the soil of the Fatherland when it becomes necessary." (Loud applause.)

Belgium has sometimes been classed with the small States determined to defend themselves to the last against an attack, but equally determined not to anticipate aggression.

This is a view that calls for correction. The moment the conflict broke out, Belgium realized that the Netherlands might be attacked while she herself was spared, at least for the time being. On several occasions—particularly at the end of October—there were grave reports which appeared to confirm this supposition. Holland appeared at that time to be in far graver danger than Belgium. On November 6th, King Leopold left for The Hague. Although his interview with Queen Wilhelmina was about the Netherlands proposal that they should renew their offer of good offices, it is significant that he was accompanied by the General who was his Military Adviser. The Government discussed the attitude to be adopted in such a contingency, but although the discussion was secret, considerable space was devoted to it in the international Press. The resolutions adopted were outlined in the Chamber on December 19th in a speech by the Minister for Foreign Affairs. " I want," said M. Spaak, " to be quite free to form a judgment in the light of all the facts. For that reason, I think it would be unwise to decide now what attitude we should have to adopt if the situation in Holland changes. But I should like to make it clear that it would be madness to suppose such an event would leave us indifferent. As far as I am concerned—and I am sure I am speaking for the whole Government—I am deeply conscious of all the ties that bind Belgium and the Netherlands " (Appendix 12). There was no doubt as to the meaning of these words. They were loudly applauded. Such an attitude fully conforms to the " policy of independence " as understood by the Belgian Government. Public opinion was almost unanimous in approving it; the Minister for Foreign Affairs, speaking in the Senate on April 17th, three weeks before the aggression, fully confirmed his earlier statements.

Was it necessary to do more ?

On several occasions Belgium believed she was on the verge of being attacked by Germany. She had been made aware that such an attack had been closely studied. She had not remained passive. She had drawn all the conclusions which her concern for her security forced upon her.

On the outbreak of the conflict, the Belgian forces were placed in such a way as to protect all the frontiers. The Government intended to act strictly in accordance with the correct and loyal attitude she had always adopted. But once a powerful German Army was concentrated near Belgian territory and the representatives of the Reich themselves seemed to think there might be an attack, the King, with the full approval of the Government, felt quite justified in diverting the whole of the Belgian forces to where the danger undoubtedly threatened. The units in the west were withdrawn and sent to the east. On several occasions, the Reich made remarks or criticisms on this subject. The Belgian Government constantly refused to take account of them, as it felt that the steps taken were fully justified by the German Army's preparations for aggression.

Belgium had yet another cause for anxiety, in addition to the impending danger. She was unable to meet aggression by herself. Great Britain and France had undertaken to assist her, but to be effective help had to be prompt. Arrangements were therefore made by the High Command for this purpose, though in keeping with the rôle Belgium had adopted. The Minister of National Defence, General Denis, gave Parliament a formal assurance. " The responsible Belgian authorities," he said, on February 7th, 1940, " will neglect no steps to enable the Powers that have guaranteed Belgium to fulfil their obligations towards us." From 1914 to 1936—twenty-two years—the Belgian General Staff maintained close contact with the French General Staff.

The Belgian Command had received from the Commander-in-Chief of the Franco-British Army an assurance that he had at his disposal everything that was necessary to ensure that the help to Belgium be rendered without delay. Events proved that he was right. On May 10th, the French and British forces took up their positions within the time-limit laid down.

Belgium was discreetly advised to seek Franco-British aid without awaiting an act of aggression. She did not accept this advice, which she regarded as incompatible with the attitude she intended loyally to maintain. Moreover, it had grave disadvantages. On several occasions, she was under the impression that preventive intervention by France and Great Britain was just what the Germans were secretly hoping for. The German Army was concentrated on the Belgian frontier, ready to launch an attack. If the French and British Armies had entered Belgian territory, the German attack would have followed immediately and the advantage gained by them would have been slight. The Government knew that these armies could not go beyond the K.W. line. To appeal for preventive aid would have entailed the occupation of half the country by the German invaders. The only result would have been to set in motion earlier the events that occurred in May. The course of these events would not have been changed, because it was due to factors outside Belgium's control. The chief cause was the great superiority which the Powers who were the guardians of peace had allowed the aggressive Powers to acquire. There was in particular the weakening of France, which, on the eve of the German aggression, manifested itself by more and more disquieting signs: a ministerial crisis, a crisis of the High Command, and the weakening of the will to conquer.

The Government could not have prevented the disasters that occurred in May, but an appeal for preventive aid would have given them an entirely different meaning and the people would have endured them with far less fortitude.

The case of Belgium would have become far less clear, and from then on would have been open to discussion. Germany, relying on the Declaration of 1937, would have represented Franco-British intervention as justifying her own aggression. She would have accused Belgium of failing to keep her promises and of being responsible for her own troubles. Towards neutral countries and towards herself Belgium would have ceased to be what she was in 1914, a loyal nation, a nation that had been attacked, though no shadow of blame attached to her.

The military defeat, the piercing of the French lines on the

3

Meuse, the subsequent enemy occupation, would not have been avoided. But Belgium would not have had the support, in these terrible trials, of the moral force generated by her attitude.

One of the chief objectives in 1936, as has been seen, was to assemble all the national forces before the danger, and so to act that the nation would arise as one man against aggression, just as it did in 1914, though this time with an infinitely more powerful and better-trained army.

This result was fully achieved. At the beginning of the conflict a Coalition Government was set up in which the three political parties were represented. The whole world heard the proud words in which the King himself gave the watchword: " If we were attacked," he said on October 27th, " —and may God preserve us from that fate—in spite of the solemn and categorical undertakings given to us in 1937 and renewed just before the war, we should fight without hesitation, but with ten times the means. And this time again the whole country would be behind the Army " (Appendix 10).

Never did foreign policy meet with such general approval in Belgium. It is only necessary to read the debates in the Senate on April 16th and 17th, three weeks before the aggression. There had been growing approval from the beginning of the conflict; even those who were formerly critical fully approved. " I am the more qualified to say what I think of this policy," said a Walloon Socialist senator, " in that I was opposed to it at the beginning. Confusing independence with neutrality, I told myself that neutrality was something shady and cowardly. But after these dreadful events which have made the human conscience bleed, I have realized that I was mistaken, and for the past eight months I have felt sure our young King was right." (Hear, hear.) " And, old republican as I am, I thank him."

The debate closed with a vote that was almost unanimous —131 for and only 3 Communists against. There were two abstentions.

The Government would not have been able to carry the

nation with it on any other policy, even if it had wanted to do so; had it tried, the attempt would have led to serious internal dissension and confusion, the consequences of which might have been fatal. National unity would have been impaired, and by that very fact the country's power of resistance would have been weakened.

On the contrary, at the moment of supreme trial, the whole country, except for a few scattered elements of little importance, was resolved and united as it had never been at any previous period of its history. The Rexist Party, which had Fascist leanings, and had had a passing success five years before, at the height of the economic depression, was completely broken up. Most of its representatives had openly supported the national union; this was also true of the Flemish nationalists, who represented the extremist element in Flemish public opinion. The fifth column was represented only by scattered individuals; it was not able to demonstrate openly.

After the German aggression, foreign observers sometimes asked the Belgians what good their policy of independence and their efforts to prevent war in their territory had done them. It is true that this policy prevented neither German aggression nor invasion. It could perhaps reduce the risk slightly, though it could not remove it. Only the foresight and armed force of the Great Powers could have done that. But Belgium's attitude and her consistency in maintaining it were nevertheless of inestimable value to her. They cemented national unity and strengthened the common will to resist at a time when the country was about to face one of the most terrible ordeals of its history: an aggression of unparalleled violence, the brutal onslaught of an unexpected and un- merited disaster, the moral torture and deprivation entailed by a new occupation, the spectre of famine. These are the fundamental safeguards which it was essential Belgium should have when her very existence was threatened by the storm.

III

THE GERMAN AGGRESSION

THE final warning came at the beginning of May. On Saturday the 4th, the Netherlands Government had news that the Netherlands would be attacked in the next few days.[1] Security measures were immediately reinforced, Army leave was stopped and men on leave were recalled. There was less tension in Belgium; public opinion was used to these continuous alarms; it was aware that every precaution had been taken, and it remained calm; security measures were ready; the authorities were able to confine themselves to recommending special vigilance.

There was no fresh information during the days of the 8th–9th. In private conversations, Axis diplomats were reassuring.

On the evening of the 9th, secret information came through that the aggression would occur at dawn on the following day. In previous months, the Belgian authorities had received similar information. At about ten o'clock, guards at different points on the frontier began to report that they could hear confused noises in German territory: footsteps, voices, motors, and moving traffic. At about eleven o'clock, the Luxemburg authorities were informed that National Socialists in the Grand Duchy had been warned.

These signs were a disquieting confirmation of the earlier information. The authorities were at once notified. At midnight the Prime Minister, the Minister of National Defence, the Minister of Justice, the Principal Private Secretary, and the Secretary of the King, the Military Attorney-General, met in the office of the Minister for Foreign Affairs, who had with him his chief collaborators. They discussed the situation quietly and awaited information. It was not the first time since the beginning of the conflict

[1] Van Kleffens, *The Rape of the Netherlands*, p. 102.

that similar circumstances had brought them together in this room in the middle of the night. Outside, the sleeping town lay silent. At about one o'clock, the Belgian Minister at Luxemburg telephoned that clashes had occurred between the police and National Socialist formations who were trying to seize by force the barriers put up on the main roads leading to the German frontier.

From two o'clock in the morning, the Dutch wireless stations announced, time after time, that aeroplanes going from east to west were flying over various localities in the Netherlands. It was impossible to ascertain the importance and significance of this information, but all the signs pointed in the same direction. The Government decided there and then to introduce a state of siege and to arrest suspected persons in the eastern provinces so as to prevent internal action against our lines of defence.

As the night wore on, there was a fairly long lull. When dawn was about to break, the peace of the capital had not been disturbed.

From 4.30 information was received which left no shadow of doubt: the hour had struck. Aircraft were first reported in the east. At five o'clock came news of the bombing of two Netherlands aerodromes, the violation of the Belgian frontier, the landing of German soldiers at the Eben-Emael Fort, the bombing of the Jemelle station.

While the Minister of National Defence was checking this information, Brussels was suddenly awakened to a radiant dawn at 5.17 a.m. by the mournful sound of the sirens, and soon the windows at the Ministry of Foreign Affairs, where the chief members of the Government were still assembled, were shaken by the firing of anti-aircraft artillery and German bombs dropped on the Evere aerodrome and on several parts of the town.

It was at once decided to appeal to Belgium's guarantors, and this was done.

At 8.30 the German Ambassador came to the Ministry of Foreign Affairs. When he entered the Minister's room, he began to take a paper from his pocket. M. Spaak stopped him: " I beg your pardon, Mr. Ambassador. I will speak first." And in an indignant voice, he read the Belgian Government's protest: " Mr. Ambassador, the German Army has just attacked our country. This is the second time in twenty-five years that Germany has committed a criminal aggression against a neutral and loyal Belgium. What has just happened is perhaps even more odious than the aggression of 1914. No ultimatum, no note, no protest of any kind has ever been placed before the Belgian Government. It is through the attack itself that Belgium has learnt that Germany has violated the undertakings given by her on October 13th, 1937, and renewed spontaneously at the beginning of the war. The act of aggression committed by Germany, for which there is no justification whatever, will deeply shock the conscience of the world. The German Reich will be held responsible by history. Belgium is resolved to defend herself. Her cause, which is the cause of Right, cannot be vanquished."

The Ambassador was then able to read the note he had brought: " I am instructed by the Government of the Reich," he said, " to make the following declaration: In order to forestall the invasion of Belgium, Holland, and Luxemburg, for which Great Britain and France have been making preparations clearly aimed at Germany, the Government of the Reich is compelled to ensure the neutrality of the three countries mentioned by means of arms. For this purpose, the Government of the Reich will bring up an armed force of the greatest size, so that resistance of any kind will be useless. The Government of the Reich guarantees Belgium's European and colonial territory, as well as her dynasty, on condition that no resistance is offered. Should there be any resistance, Belgium will risk the destruction of her country and the loss of her independence. It is therefore in the interests of Belgium that the population be called upon to cease all resistance and that the authorities be given the necessary instructions to make contact with the German Military Command."

In the middle of this communication, M. Spaak, who had

by his side the Secretary-General of the Department, interrupted the Ambassador: " Hand me the document," he said. " I should like to spare you so painful a task." After studying the note, M. Spaak confined himself to pointing out that he had already replied by the protest he had just made.

During the morning, a fuller note of protest was addressed to the representatives of all the foreign Governments (Appendix 17). Most of them, though neutrals, at once informed Belgium of their sympathy.

In the note which the German Government instructed the German Ambassador to hand in, no definite complaint was made to justify the aggression against Belgium. At the very moment when her aeroplanes were bombing peaceful sleeping citizens, Germany once again represented herself as the protector of their neutrality. Already, however, the German News Service (D.N.B.) had forwarded a communication throwing responsibility for the invasion on the victim. Later on, the Reich published a White Book containing charges of alleged collusion between Belgium, Great Britain, and France. Of the twenty documents reproduced, there are only two which come from a Belgian military authority. They relate to operations to be carried out on Belgian or Dutch territories; but all of them are purely defensive, and they are clearly intended to deal with German aggression against Belgium and Holland.

On the basis of the declarations of the Minister of National Defence in the Chamber on February 7th, 1940, the German Government accused the Belgian Government of organizing her defences exclusively against the Reich. The open threats against Belgium from the end of October 1939 amply justified the decision of the High Command to draw up the Army along the frontier, where preparations for an attack were being made. The plan of these preparations had fallen into the hands of the Belgian authorities at the beginning of January. This document, three-parts burnt, is attached (Appendix 13). It is undoubtedly of an aggressive nature. The offensive manœuvres which were to be carried out by the German western army were not intended to counter an invasion of Belgium by French and British forces; they were designed, on the contrary, to crush the Belgian Army before Allied help could arrive.

The document, about which the German Government has never been able to furnish any explanation, definitively settles the question of responsibility.

In any case, there could be no justification, in Belgium's view, for the surprise attack made on the country at dawn, when official relations between the two countries were quite normal. Belgium knew she was innocent. When the fight began, the King was able to remind his people of the Belgium of 1914, and to show that now as then she was resolute and blameless.

" For the second time in a quarter of a century," he said, " Belgium—a neutral and loyal country—has been attacked by the German Empire in spite of the most solemn undertakings contracted before the whole world. The Belgian people, who are fundamentally peaceful, have done everything in their power to prevent this, but between sacrifice and dishonour the Belgian of 1940 hesitates no more than did the Belgian of 1914. . . . France and Great Britain have promised to help us. Their advance troops are already pushing forward to join up with ours. The fight will be hard. Great sacrifices and deprivation will be asked of you, but there can be no doubt about the final victory. I intend to remain faithful to my constitutional oath to maintain the independence and integrity of the territory. Like my father in 1914, I have put myself at the head of our Army with the same faith, with the same clear conscience. The cause of Belgium is pure. With the help of God it will triumph " (Appendix 18).

The Council of Ministers met at the beginning of the morning and were informed of the events of the night before and of the appeal addressed immediately to the guarantor Powers. Parliament met in the afternoon. It approved unanimously the steps taken by the Government to meet the aggression.

No doubt the nation had hoped to the end that Belgium would be spared war, but during those long months on the brink of danger, it had become familiar with the idea that the fateful hour might strike at any time. It remained calm and well-disciplined. Everyone did his duty.

The German air-raid shortly after dawn caused many deaths. A Government declaration emphasized that Brussels was an open town and that there were no troops there. The Belgian Ambassador in London was instructed at the same time to ask urgently for immediate aid from the British Air Force.

From an early hour, there was violent fighting on the frontier. It was learnt that, taking advantage of a surprise attack at the end of the night, air-borne detachments played an important rôle. The public became obsessed with the idea of parachutists. Nowhere inside the country, however, did enemy agents dare—as in the Grand Duchy of Luxemburg and on an even more extensive scale in Norway and Holland—to commit acts of sabotage or violence.

Only one thing mattered: the defence at all costs of Belgium's independence. It seemed incredible that there could be any doubt as to the attitude to be adopted. As those who some years earlier had defined Belgium's position had hoped, duty was quite clear to all, in the light of the facts.

IV

HOW THE BELGIAN ARMY DEFENDED
THE TERRITORY

Now it was for the Army to make its stand against aggression and to fulfil the mission Belgium had undertaken. On behalf of neighbouring countries, as well as for her own sake, she had undertaken " to defend with all her forces the frontiers of Belgium against any aggression or invasion and to prevent Belgian territory from being used for the passage of troops or as a base of operations for aggression against another State."

After mobilization, the Army available for carrying out this mission consisted of:

5 Regular Army Corps and 2 Reserve Army Corps consisting in all of:

12 Regular Infantry Divisions.
2 Divisions of " Chasseurs Ardennais."
6 Reserve Infantry Divisions.
1 Brigade of Cyclist Frontier Guards.

1 Cavalry Corps of 2 Cavalry Divisions and 1 Brigade of Motorized Cavalry.

2 Reconnaissance Regiments (Gendarmerie).
4 Air Force Regiments.
2 Anti-Aircraft Artillery Regiments.
4 Army Artillery Regiments.
Army Troops (Engineers, Signals, etc.).
Fortress Troops.
Services.

The Belgian plan, *in the event of a German aggression,* provided for:

(*a*) A delaying position along the Albert Canal from Antwerp to Liège and the Meuse from Liège to Namur, which was to be held long enough to allow French and

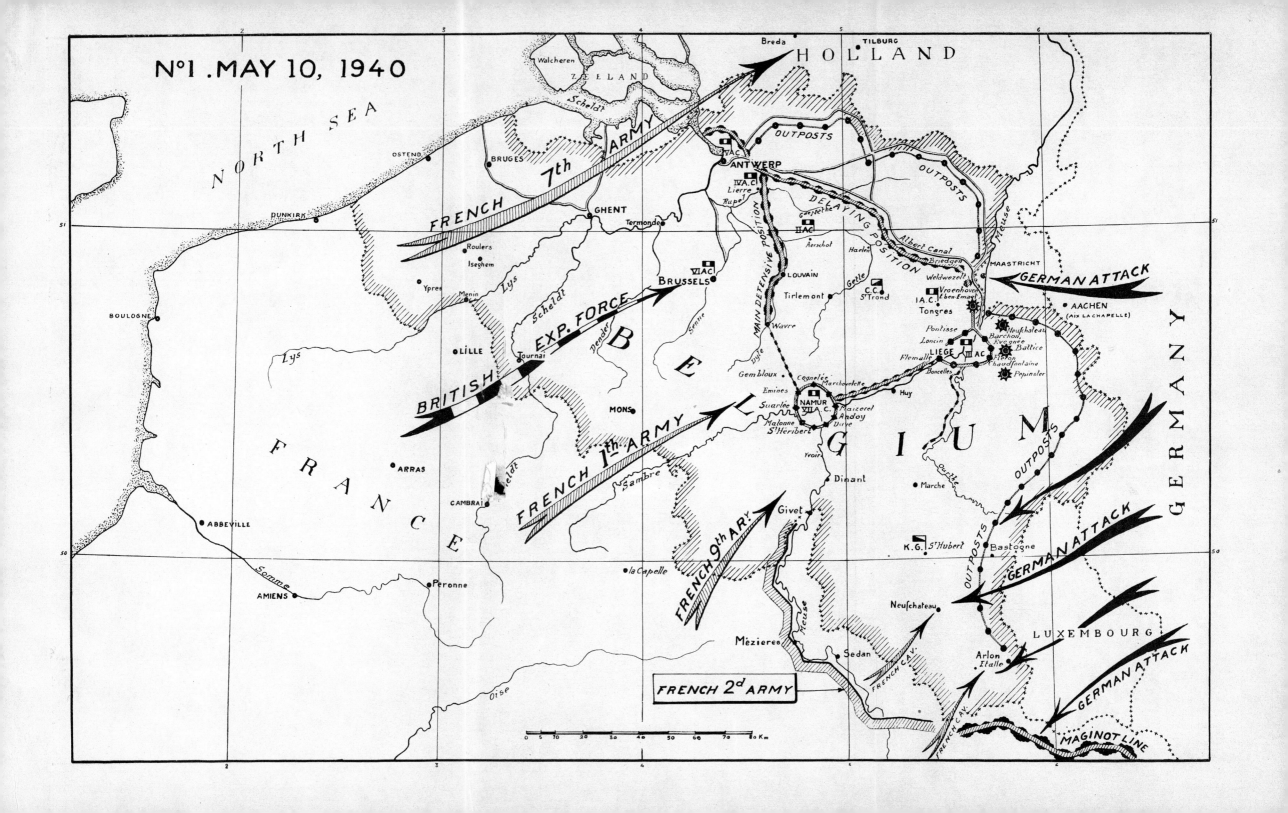

British troops to occupy the line Antwerp–Namur–Givet.[1] It was anticipated that the forces of the guarantor Powers would be in action on the third day of invasion.

(b) Withdrawal to the Antwerp–Namur position.

(c) The Belgian Army was to hold the sector—exclusive Louvain, inclusive Antwerp—as part of the main Allied defensive position.

During the evening of May 9th, the Belgian Military Attaché in Berlin intimated that the Germans intended to attack on the following day. Offensive preparations and troop movements on the Belgian frontier confirmed this information.

May 10*th.*—At ten minutes past twelve (midnight) on May 10th, General Headquarters gave the alarm. For the third time since mobilization had taken place, the Belgian troops took up their war stations (Map 1).

At *four o'clock*, without ultimatum or declaration of war, a powerful German Air Force bombed and machine-gunned the aerodromes, stations, and communication centres. The Belgian Air Force, taken by surprise, lost over half its machines on the ground.

FIRST PHASE: DEFENCE OF THE DELAYING POSITION AND WITHDRAWAL TO THE MAIN POSITION ANTWERP–NAMUR

May 10*th*–13*th* (Maps 1, 2, and 3).—An unusually daring *coup de main* was carried out on the front Eben-Emael–Vroenhoven–Veldwezelt–Briedgen (Map 2), where one salient of our defensive position skirting the frontier of Holland could not be covered by outposts. Troops transported by gliders were landed behind the bridges of Vroenhoven, Veldwezelt, and Briedgen, whilst German

---

[1] It should be noted that, in accordance with the accepted principle of the Belgian Army, there was only one order—to resist to the end.

Chapter V, "The Defensive and Retreat," Article 168 of the Belgian Field Service Regulations prescribes that: "In the event of an attack, it shall be compulsory to resist to the end. The Commander-in-Chief alone shall reach a decision as to the expediency of ceasing resistance on any position and as to the moment at which it should cease."

aircraft incessantly bombarded the whole of the sector. The glider troops, reinforced by parachutists, surprised the detachments guarding the bridges and captured them from the rear. The artillery of the fort of Eben-Emael, covering these bridges, had already been put out of action by a new method of warfare. A few gliders, taking advantage of the dark, landed on the roof of the fort. Their crews succeeded, by means of explosives, in putting out of action or damaging the defensive armament of the fort.

Transport aircraft showered parachutists on Eben-Emael. These parachutists established themselves on the fort, entered through the breaches, and began to destroy the galleries, while the aerial bombardment was continued, with redoubled intensity, on neighbouring units of the fort, and especially on the artillery, so as to prevent them from giving any help.

The Belgian Army could not by itself fulfil its mission of throwing back the aggressor. In their Declaration on April 24th, 1937, Great Britain and France had confirmed their promise to assist Belgium, as provided in the Locarno agreements. While the fort of Eben-Emael and the neighbouring units were fully engaged in battle, in very difficult circumstances, the Government appealed to the guarantor Powers.

In an Order of the Day, General Gamelin said: " The attack we have been expecting since last October began this morning."

As promised by the Minister of National Defence in Parliament on February 7th, the authorities had neglected no step to enable the guarantor Powers to fulfil their obligations. Our southern frontier was opened to the French and British Armies, which were to occupy the positions assigned to them, according to a carefully thought-out plan.

The heads of motorized columns of the Seventh French Army (General Giraud) began an advance into Holland in the direction of Breda and Tilburg to defend the mouths of the Scheldt and Zeeland.

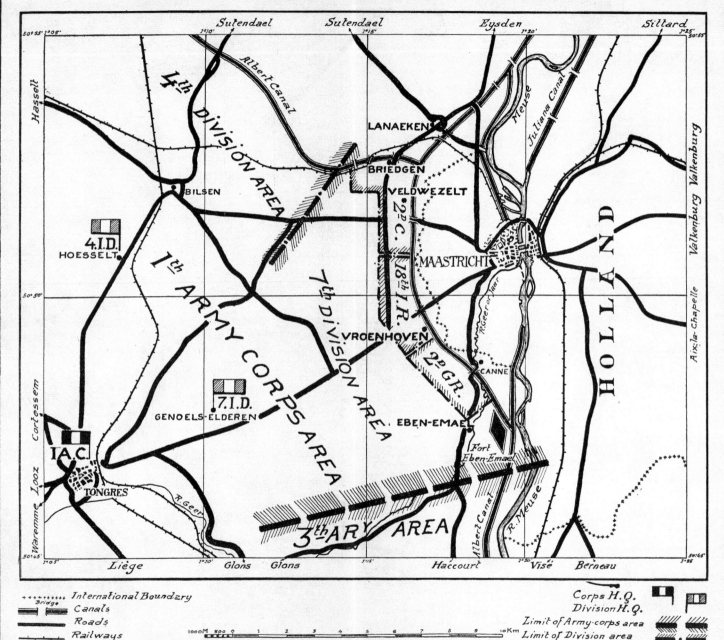

Nº 2. MAY 10, 1940
EBEN-EMAEL-VROENHOVEN-VELDWEZELT-BRIEGDEN

Sutendael
Sutendael
Eysden
Sittard

Hasselt

4th DIVISION AREA

Albert Canal

LANAEKEN

Meuse

Juliana Canal

Bilsen

BRIEGDEN
VELDWEZELT

4. I.D.
HOESSELT

1th ARMY CORPS AREA

7th DIVISION AREA

2ᵈ C.

18th I.R.

MAASTRICHT

HOLLAND

R. Geer or Jaer

VROENHOVEN

2ᵈ GR.

7. I.D.
GENOELS-ELDEREN

CANNE

EBEN-EMAEL

I.A.C.

TONGRES

R. Geer

Fort Eben-Emael

Albert Canal

R. Meuse

3th ARY AREA

Waremme Looz Cortessem

Liège
Glons
Glons
Haccourt
Visé
Berneau

Aix-la-Chapelle
Valkenburg Valkenburg

International Boundary
Bridge
Canals
Roads
Railways

Corps H.Q.
Division H.Q.
Limit of Army corps area
Limit of Division area

1000M 500 0   1   2   3   4   5   6   7   8   9   10Km

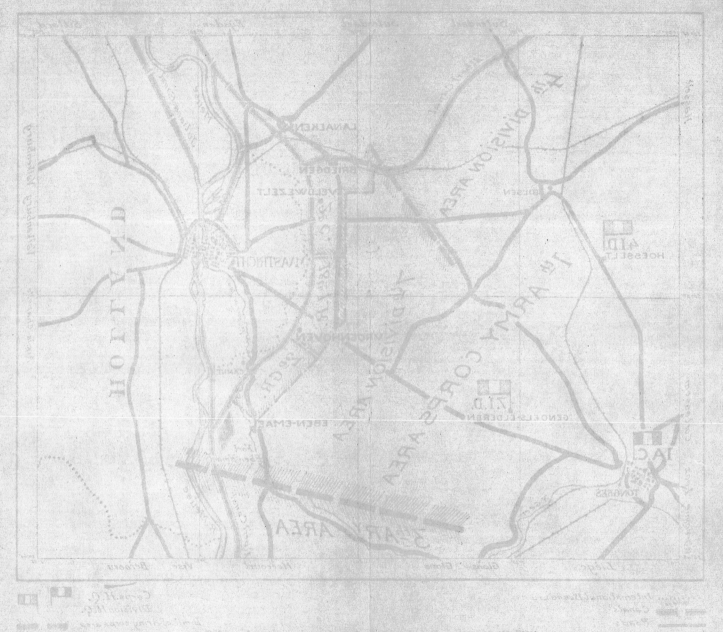

In the evening mobile troops of the B.E.F. (General Gort) took up a position on the Dyle between Wavre and Louvain, while the Prioux Cavalry Corps, preceding the First French Army (General Blanchard) reached the Wavre–Namur line. A group of light divisions belonging to the Second French Army (General Huntzinger) advanced into Belgian Luxemburg in the direction of Marche, Bastogne, and Arlon. It encountered strong enemy resistance, and was brought back in the evening to the Etalle–Neufchâteau line.

The light troops of the Ninth French Army (General Corap) reached the Ourthe cutting (see Map 1).

Early on the morning of May 10th, the King had gone to his General Headquarters at Breendonck, near Antwerp.

May 11th.—By taking the bridges at Vroenhoven, Veldwezelt, and Briedgen, and putting the fort of Eben-Emael out of action, the enemy obtained a footing on the left bank of the Albert Canal on the front held by the 7th Infantry Division.

The regiments in this division (2nd Grenadier Regiment at Canne, 18th of the Line at Vroenhoven, 2nd Carabineers at Veldwezelt–Briedgen) held on to their positions desperately. In spite of an aerial bombardment of unparalleled violence, in spite of disorganization in the rear and of the disorganization caused by enemy parachutists, there were many counter-attacks for the purpose of retaking the bridges. By dint of heroic efforts, the bridge at Briedgen was retaken and destroyed. But the enemy had had time to establish firmly anchored bridgeheads at Vroenhoven and Veldwezelt. His supporting fire and still more his fighter aircraft tied down the Belgian battalions and inflicted heavy losses on them. The intervention of our reserves and motorized troops recalled from the Ardennes did not succeed in restoring the situation. A Belgian squadron, offering itself up as a sacrifice, flew over and bombed the bridge of Vroenhoven: eleven machines out of twelve were brought down.

There was no response, up to midday, to the requests addressed to the British and French Commands asking for bomber aircraft. It was not until the morning of May 12th that the R.A.F. set out on its expedition to bomb the Maastricht bridges.

From the very beginning, the German Air Force had an overwhelming superiority. There was never to be an opportunity of wresting from it, even locally, the mastery of the air. Its action was favoured by specially good weather conditions throughout the eighteen days of the campaign. For eighteen days the Belgian Army had the depressing feeling that it was manœuvring and fighting under a sky that belonged exclusively to the enemy.

After resisting desperately for thirty-six hours, the 7th Infantry Division withdrew. The fort of Eben-Emael fell. The enemy armoured divisions hurled through the gap, advanced beyond Tongres, threatening to envelop the whole of the Albert Canal position and the fortified town of Liège. The withdrawal of the 7th Infantry Division was followed by that of the 4th Infantry Division on its left.

May 12th.—On the evening of May 11th, the High Command decided to withdraw our troops behind the Antwerp–Namur line.

Beginning on the night of May 11th–12th, our forces deployed on the Albert Canal and the Meuse gradually withdrew, covered by a network of demolitions and by rearguards posted astride Tongres, then on the line of the Gette.

During the day of May 12th, there was a conference between King Leopold, General Van Overstraeten, M. Daladier, General Georges, General Billotte, General Champon, and General Pownall, Chief of the British General Staff, at the Château of Casteau, near Mons. The King and General Pownall agreed that General Billotte, commanding the French Northern Army Group, should be delegated by General Georges [1] " to ensure that the operations of the Allied Armies in Belgium and Holland were co-ordinated."

The *Belgian Army* reorganized in order to range itself in good order on the prepared position from Antwerp to

[1] General Georges commanded the North-Eastern Army Group, that is all the French and British Forces opposite the German frontier.

Louvain.   The Third Army Corps had evacuated the fortified
town of Liège in order to escape being encircled.   But the
forts, with the exception of Eben-Emael, held on and acted
as strong-points, hindering the invader's communications.

Colonel Modart, one of the defenders of Loncin in 1914,
who was now commanding the Liège Fortress Regiment,
followed General Leman's example, and shut himself up in
the Flemalle fort to direct and to put heart into the defence.

The *British Army* had three divisions in position on the
Louvain–Wavre front.   Six other divisions were echeloned
in depth between the Dyle and the Scheldt.

The *First French Army*, covered in the direction of Tirle-
mont-Huy by a cavalry corps, reached its dispositions on
the Wavre–Gembloux–Namur front.

The Namur position, defended by the Seventh Belgian
Army Corps (8th Infantry Division, 2nd Division of " Chasseurs Ardennais," 12th French Infantry Division), absorbed
also the troops of the Keyaerts group (1st Division of
" Chasseurs Ardennais "), who fought a delaying action
throughout the whole depth of the Ardennes and did
considerable demolition work.

In the south, the *Ninth French Army* established itself
on the Meuse from Namur to Mézières.   In *Holland*, the
situation was not clear.   Air-borne troops which landed at
The Hague and at Rotterdam paralysed the defence,
preventing the Allies from making contact with the main
Netherlands forces.   The Seventh French Army was faced
by superior forces which emerged from the Peel marshes.

In short, in spite of the fall of Eben-Emael and the loss
of two bridges, the Belgian Army carried out the only
independent mission for which it was responsible—it held
on to the Liège and Albert Canal position for long enough
to enable the bulk of the Allied forces to occupy the Antwerp–
Namur–Givet line.

In accordance with the decisions reached at Casteau, it
was henceforward to take part in the general plan of the
Allied forces.

May 13*th* (Map 3).—While the greater part of the Belgian

Army, already in position, feverishly organized the defence of the Antwerp–Louvain position, detachments of our cavalry corps posted as rearguards on the Gette were responsible for covering the withdrawal of our rearmost divisions. Violent fighting took place at Haelen and Tirlemont, where the 2nd Regiment of Guides and the 1st and 2nd Carabineer Cyclists particularly distinguished themselves.

The King issued the following proclamation to the troops:

" SOLDIERS,

" The Belgian Army, brutally assailed by an unparalleled surprise attack, grappling with forces that are better equipped and have the advantage of a formidable air force, has for three days carried out difficult operations, the success of which is of the utmost importance to the general conduct of the battle and to the result of the war.

" These operations require from all of us—officers and men—exceptional efforts, sustained day and night, despite a moral tension tested to its limits by the sight of the devastation wrought by a pitiless invader.

" However severe the trial may be, you will come through it gallantly.

" Our position improves with every hour; our ranks are closing up. In the critical days that are ahead of us, you will summon up all your energies, you will make every sacrifice, to stem the invasion.

" Just as they did in 1914 on the Yser, so now the French and British troops are counting on you: the safety and honour of the country are in your hands.

" LEOPOLD."

Alarming news came from the French front. At seven o'clock the Germans had attacked the Ninth French Army at Houx—where only the advanced troops were in position —and infiltrated into the valley of the Meuse from Yvoir to Givet. An enemy attack supported by artillery and a very powerful air force on the Second Army front seized

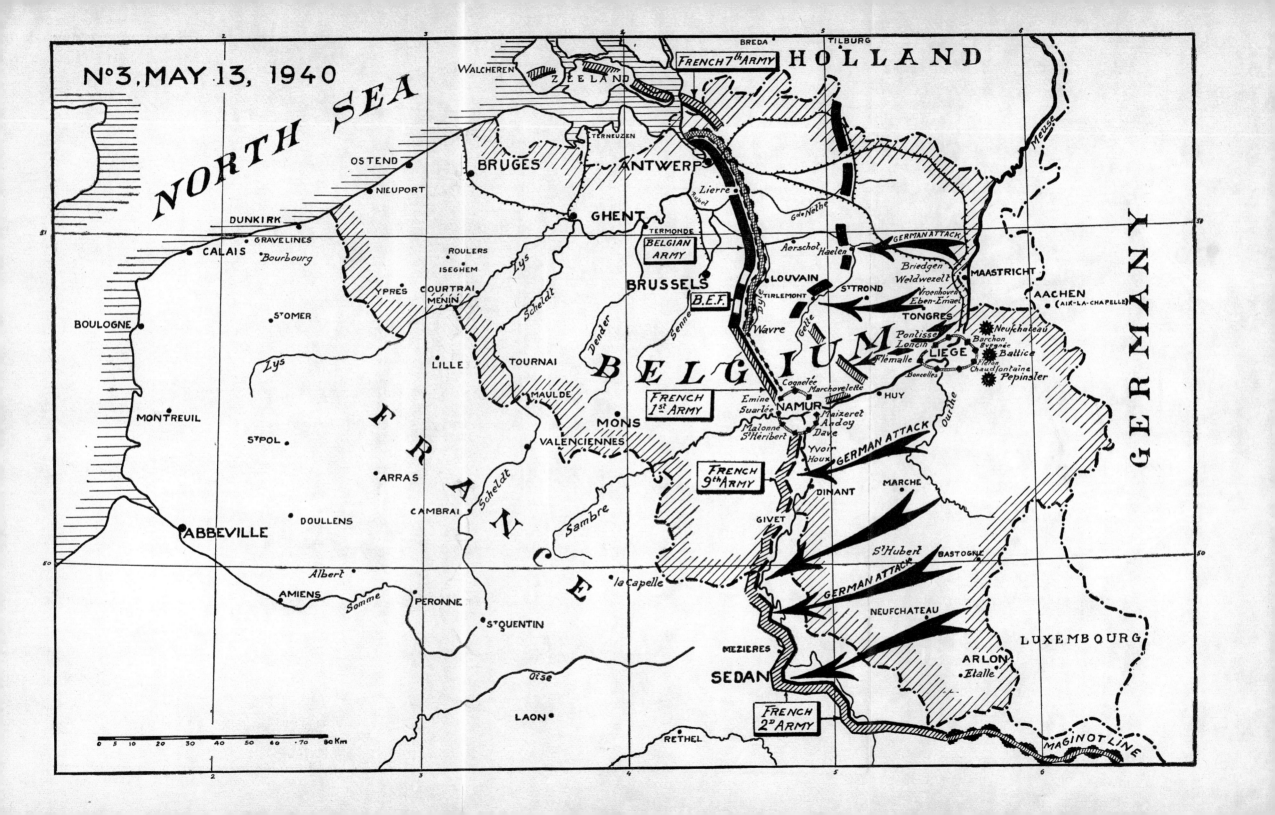

Sedan at 5 p.m. and made a breach in which a formidable mass of armoured divisions concentrated. Was not the German attack to the north of the Meuse simply a diversion to deprive the Allied centre of its reserves?

SECOND PHASE: THE BREAK-THROUGH AT SEDAN AND THE GERMAN PUSH TO THE CHANNEL, INVOLVING THE ABANDONMENT OF THE ANTWERP–NAMUR POSITION, *May* 14*th to* 20*th.* (Map No. 4)

May 14*th,* 15*th, and* 16*th.*—Confining itself to exerting a firm pressure on the Belgian–British front, the enemy directed its main effort against the French Armies.

Between the Sambre and the Meuse, the French Ninth Army broke up in disorder. General Giraud, who had just been given the Command, was captured on the 16th at La Capelle.

The irresistible drive of the Panzer Divisions thrown into the Sedan breach seriously threatened to envelop the whole of the Allied troops engaged in Belgium. This led the Commander-in-Chief of the Allied Armies on the evening of the 15th to a decision which had very important results—the abandonment of the Antwerp–Namur position and a withdrawal behind the Escaut; that is to say, the abandonment, without any real resistance, of a powerfully organized position and the taking up of an improvised position.

The fortified position of Namur, isolated by the French withdrawal, was abandoned. The forts, as at Liège, acted as strong-points and held up the enemy's advance. The withdrawal of the Seventh Belgian Army Corps, which was endangered by the speed with which the French withdrew, was only possible thanks to the skilful dispositions of its Commander, General Deffontaine.

The Seventh French Army, unable by its offensive in Zeeland to prevent the capitulation of the Netherlands Army, fell back in disorder on Antwerp. Most of it was diverted as reinforcements in the direction of the First Army.

The magnificent resistance put up by the Liège forts was

4

recognized by this message from the King on the 16th:
" Colonel Modart, commanding the Liège Fortress
Regiment. Officers, non-commissioned officers and men
of the Liège fortifications, resist to the last for your country.
" I am proud of you.
" LEOPOLD."

The resistance put up by the Liège and Namur forts came
up to the expectations of the King and the Army. The fort
of Chaudfontaine did not fall until the 17th, Pontisse and
Barchon until the 18th, Evegnee until the 19th, Neufchâteau
until the 21st, Pepinster (Commandant A. Devos) was still
holding out on the 28th.

At Namur, the fort of Marchovelette fell on the 18th,
Suarlee on the 19th, St. Heribert and Malonne on the 21st,
Dave, Maizeret, and Andoy on the 23rd.

May 17th to 20th (Map 4).—During the night of the
16th–17th, the French and British withdrew behind the
Willebroeck Canal.

In the general retreat, the Belgian Army withdrew, step
by step, to Ghent and Termonde in three phases:

(*a*) Behind the Willebroeck Canal.

(*b*) Behind the Dendre.

(*c*) Behind the Scheldt.

Violent fighting took place on the Nethe, the Rupel, the
Willebroeck Canal, the Scheldt, Flanders Head, and on the
Dendre. During the fighting, the Belgian artillery gave
many proofs of its worth.

For three days—from May 18th to 20th—our divisions,
disposed in good order on the Escaut and the Ghent
bridgehead, held out against every attack, while the
manœuvre which was to end in the breaking up of the
Allied armies into two groups was developing on the Oise.

The British communiqué of May 21st paid tribute to the
bearing of the Belgian Army in these words:

" The Belgian Army has contributed largely towards the
success of the defensive battle now being fought."

On the evening of the 18th, the Panzer Divisions

approached Peronne. There was nothing to stop their rapid advance. The King had warned his Ministers that a final breach of the Allied front was not impossible, and that this would lead to the isolation of the Belgian Army and part of the French and British Armies, and might have serious consequences, that is to say, capitulation.

On the 19th, M. Gutt, Minister of Finance, who was on a mission to Paris, drew the attention of M. Reynaud, President of the Council, to the growing danger to the Belgian Army, which was exposed to envelopment with all its consequences. He pressed for urgent decisions by the High Command in order to avert the impending disaster.

On May 20th, hearing of the fall of Cambrai and of the German threat to Abbeville, and aware of the state of exhaustion of the French northern forces, the King informed London of his anxiety.

THIRD PHASE: ATTEMPT TO COUNTER-ATTACK TO REUNITE
THE ALLIED FRONT. MISSION OF THE BELGIAN ARMY:
TO COVER THIS OPERATION BY DEFENDING THE LYS ON
A FRONT EXTENDED FROM 50 TO 90 KM. (*May 20th
to 24th*)

May 21st.—On May 21st, the Germans entered Amiens and Montreuil: a strategic situation of the utmost gravity was thus created. It was in these dramatic circumstances that General Weygand, recalled from Syria, succeeded General Gamelin as Commander-in-Chief of the Allied Armies.

Exposed to the full onslaught of the enemy, the British left the Escaut and fell back to the Lys, and this compelled us to take a new line on the Lys, while at the same time we had to protect ourselves from Walcheren Island, which had fallen on the 19th.

On the same day, the Allied Commanders-in-Chief held a conference at Ypres. General Weygand's plan for a double counter-attack to restore the Allied front on the Arras-Albert line was discussed. It was agreed that the Belgian Army should extend its front in order to release some of the British troops to take part in these operations. The Belgian Army was also to cover these operations by holding the line of the Lys, extending in the north to the mouth of the Escaut, and eventually to withdraw to the Yser.

May 22nd.—The French and British attempts to re-establish contact with their armies on the Somme drew the bulk of their forces in the direction of Arras. Twice the Belgian front was weakened by an extension to the south, and on May 22nd it held a front over 90 km. long.

The Franco-British attack under command of General Blanchard made some progress. The French light mechanized units reached the Sensee, in the direction of Cambrai, but their thrust was broken by the German Panzer Divisions.

At the same time, south of the Somme, General Georges was preparing to attack north.

From north to south, the dispositions of the Belgian Forces were, first the Cavalry Corps which held the advanced position at Terneuzen, then from north to south ranged side by side the Fifth, Second, Sixth, Seventh, and Fourth Army Corps. One reserve division guarded the coast.

In reserve our First Corps had only two incomplete divisions which had been sorely tried during the preceding encounters. The 60th French Division with two regiments held the Leopold Canal in the district north of Bruges behind our Cavalry Corps.

Acting on our own authority, we sent the Sixteenth French Corps to hold the canal from Gravelines to St. Omer, in order to secure the Lys and ensure freedom of action for the Allied withdrawal in the south.

In these circumstances, the Belgian Army once again accepted battle. Whilst the armoured divisions were reported to be at Boulogne and then at St. Omer and the French and British were trying to re-establish the connection between Cambrai and Peronne, our troops held out courageously, so as to give the necessary time and space for this decisive operation.

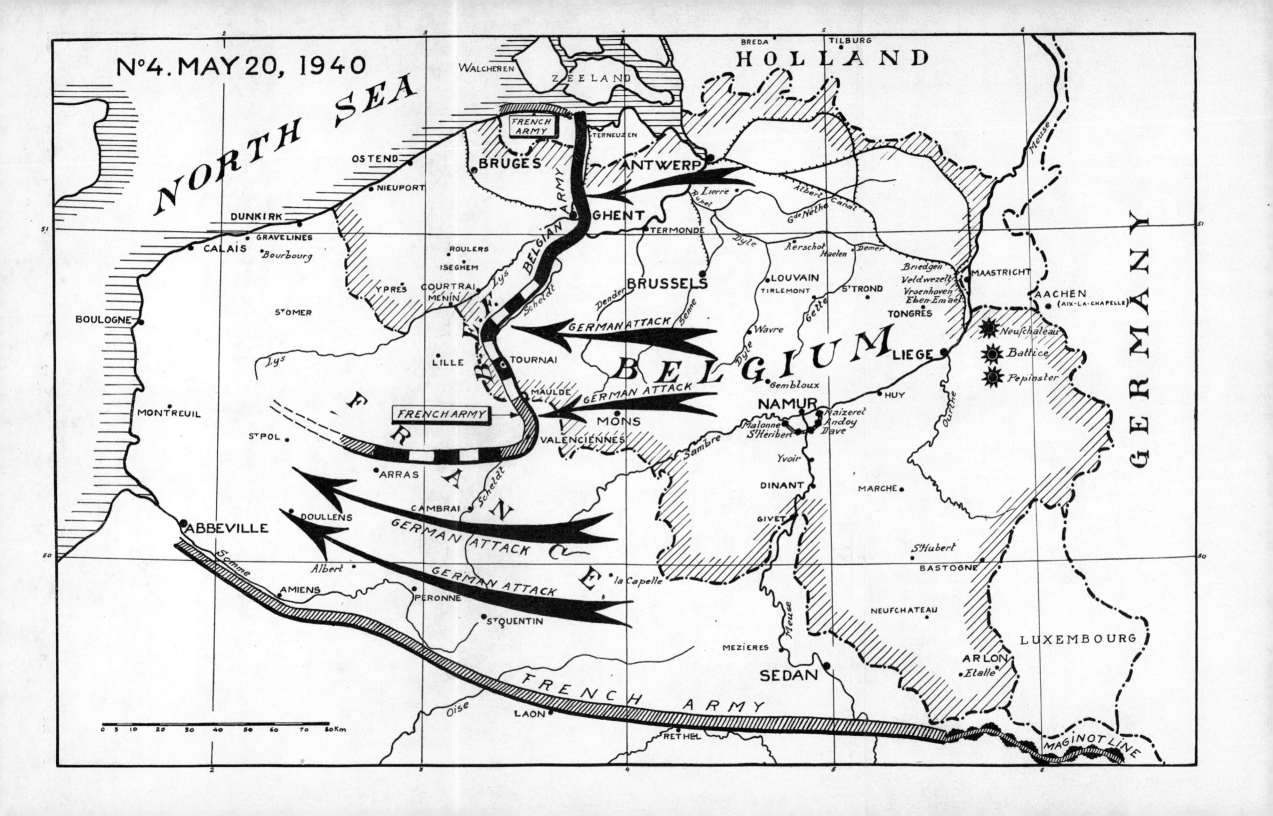

NO4. MAY 20, 1940

It was the Belgian Army, however, which was to bear the chief weight of the German forces in Belgium.

The picture would be incomplete if we did not mention the complications due to a number of motor convoys and movements of all kinds crowded along the French frontier, which was more often closed than open; the congestion caused by hundreds of thousands of refugees moving hither and thither in search of a safe area, and by bombardments which laid waste the whole of the coastal area.

May 23rd.—General Blanchard's offensive had been halted; it could not be resumed. In the south, General Georges' offensive had been stopped on the Somme: everywhere the Germans maintained their positions on the north bank of the river. It became obvious that the counterattack planned by General Weygand could not be carried out. Similarly, a second counter-attack towards Abbeville on the same day failed.

Enemy pressure compelled the Belgians to abandon Terneuzen and Ghent. The British attempt to break through at Arras had failed. The French units were not in a condition to attack.

On the other hand, motorized detachments from Boulogne and St. Pol threatened the rear of the Allies. The encircling movement was rapidly closing in. In the air, the situation was becoming increasingly difficult. Most of the airfields in the north-east of France were occupied by the enemy. There was no direct contact, and the only means of communication with the R.A.F. and the French Air Force was by wireless.

The Belgian Army was no longer allowed to use the bases at Gravelines, Dunkirk, and Bourbourg which had been placed at its disposal, and had only the ports of Ostend and Nieuport left. It was compelled to move its reserves of food, ammunition, and oil, as well as its hospital trains, along one of the few railway lines still usable.

May 24th.—A heavy German attack forced a crossing over the Lys on both sides of Courtrai on the front held by the 1st and 3rd Divisions. The great battle had begun.

Our 10th and 9th Divisions intervened and filled the gap, in spite of the enemy's violent air attacks. Two hundred prisoners were captured in a counter-attack on the front of the Second Army Corps. Our Intelligence established the fact that the attacking force consisted of four regular divisions. The Belgian artillery displayed the greatest activity in harassing the enemy day and night at all ranges. To break down this stubborn resistance, the German General Staff decided to resort to a mass air attack. Formations of over fifty bombers, protected over the coast by fighters, continuously bombed and machine-gunned our lines, our batteries, our headquarters, and our transports, preparing the way for a deadly infantry attack employing the tactics of infiltration. Unfortunately, in spite of our earnest entreaties, our troops never had the benefit of any appreciable help from the Allied air forces.

On May 24th, the enemy brought into line a fresh division from Menin to Ypres which threatened to cut us off from the British. Our 2nd Cavalry Division and our 6th Infantry Division were brought round from our left to our right and frustrated this attempt. In conjunction with the 10th Infantry Division, they kept the assailant at bay on the Ypres–Roulers line.

Twice during the 24th, M. Gutt, Minister of Finance, who had moved from Paris to London, saw Lord Halifax, Minister for Foreign Affairs, and considered with him what measures could be taken to deal with the critical situation in which the Belgian Army was now placed.

FOURTH PHASE: FAILURE OF THE COUNTER-OFFENSIVE AND ALLIED RETREAT TO DUNKIRK. RESISTANCE OF THE BELGIAN ARMY ON THE LYS UNTIL ITS MEANS WERE EXHAUSTED, *May* 25*th to* 27*th*. (Map No. 5)

May 25th.—The counter-offensive designed to break the envelopment having failed, the British troops, set free by the extension of the Belgian front which was agreed upon at the conference in Ypres on the 21st, withdrew to Dunkirk.

The vice in which the British, French, and Belgian forces were held continued to close in. From this moment, the fate of the Belgian Army was in no doubt. All hope of saving it disappeared. On the preceding days, the Germans had scattered through the Belgian lines pamphlets inviting the soldiers to lay down their arms. A rough map gave a striking illustration of their desperate situation. " In any case," said the wording, " the war is over for you. Your leaders are about to escape by air. Throw down your arms ! " (Appendix 19.)

The only object of continuing the fight was to try to save part of the Allied troops by embarking them at Dunkirk. At dawn on May 25th, the King informed first his Ministers and then his Army of his unshakable determination to resist to the limit of his forces and to share in the fate of his soldiers. His Order of the Day to the troops was as follows :

" SOLDIERS,
        " The great battle which we have been expecting has begun. It will be fierce. We will fight on with all our strength and with supreme energy.
" It is being fought on the ground where in 1914 we victoriously held the invader.
" SOLDIERS,
        " Belgium expects you to do honour to her Flag.
" OFFICERS, SOLDIERS,
        " Whatever may happen, I shall share your fate.
" I call on you all for firmness, discipline, and confidence.
" Our cause is just and pure.
" Providence will help us.
        " LONG LIVE BELGIUM!
                                        " LEOPOLD."
" IN THE FIELD, *May 25th*, 1940."

He sent a straightforward message to London describing the imminent danger and his own intentions. The death of General Billotte, representative of the Commander-in-Chief in the north, and the actual breakdown of communications with France, prevented him from sending a similar notification to Paris. But in Paris, as in London, the Ministers described the situation which was causing them the gravest anxiety.

When General Sir John Dill visited G.H.Q. on May 25th, his attention was drawn to the possibility of a break-through west of Menin, towards Ypres and Dunkirk, and to its dangers. Furthermore, at about six in the evening Colonel Davy, Head of the British Military Mission to G.H.Q., was informed that the Belgian Army would henceforward be quite unable to extend its front any farther.

May 26th.—During the night of the 25th–26th and the day of the 26th, 2,000 wagons were brought up and placed end to end to form an anti-tank barrier on the railway line from Roulers to Ypres.

The front was giving way at Iseghem, Nevele, and Ronsele; the First Division of " Chasseurs Ardennais " restored the position by bitter fighting at Nevele and Vynckt, but suddenly the battle extended to the north of Eecloo. The Germans forced a crossing over the canal at Balgerhoeck. For a moment contact with the British to the west of Menin was lost. The last reserves were assembled, the defence of the coast was taken over by Lines of Communication troops, the defence of the Yser towards the south-west, carried out up to this time by the 15th Division, was now undertaken by units that were exhausted. Auxiliary troops formed a barrier in the rear with 75-mm. guns taken from training centres.

On May 26th at midday, the Belgian Command handed the Head of the French Mission a note on the situation of the Belgian Army which said :

" The Belgian Command asks you to inform the Commander-in-Chief of the Allied Armies that the Belgian Army is in a serious situation and that the Commander-in-Chief intends to carry on the fight as long as his resources permit. The enemy is at present attacking from Eecloo to Menin; the Army has nearly reached the limits of its endurance."

No reply to this message was received from the Commander-in-Chief.

At six o'clock in the evening General Blanchard arrived to present himself to the King as successor to General Billotte. He announced that the British were evacuating the frontier position on our right and were withdrawing farther to the rear on the Lille–Ypres line. All that could be spared to fill the gap thus left between them and the Belgians was a small light mechanized division with about fifteen tanks. Moreover, in the absence of contact with General Gort, there was no means of knowing his intentions.

On the other hand, the Belgian Command handed to the Head of the Belgian Mission with British G.H.Q. the following note:

" To-day, May 26th, a very violent attack was launched against the Belgian Army on the Menin–Nevele front, and at the present moment fighting is continuing throughout the whole of the Eecloo region. In the absence of Belgian reserves, we cannot extend the boundary notified yesterday any farther to the right. We are compelled regretfully to say that we have no longer any forces available to bar the way from Ypres. Furthermore, to retreat to the Yser is impossible, since it would, without loss to the enemy, destroy our fighting units even more rapidly than if we stand and fight. Flooding of the Yser-Yperlee region has not yet been begun. The ditches of the drainage-works on the eastern bank have been filled.[1] All the preparatory work for flooding has been completed. The order to flood the eastern bank of the Yser, and the Yperlee, was given at nine o'clock on May 26th. It should be noted that flooding will be fairly slow, as this is the season of low tides. Until further instructions, there will be no flooding to the north of the Passchendael Canal."

In the evening, the King decided to make arrangements for establishing his G.H.Q. at Middelkerke, a seaside resort

[1] The order to prepare the flooding of the Yser had been given on May 19th. On the 26th, the soaked ground on the east bank was sufficient to stop tanks. All the bridges over the Yser were prepared for destruction.

a few kilometres from Ostend, and an advanced echelon of G.H.Q. established itself there on the 27th.

May 27th (Map No. 5).—Twenty-four hours earlier, the Belgian Command had suggested that the British should counter-attack between the Lys and the Escaut on the flank and rear of the German attacking force. The British Command replied that the expeditionary force was not in a fit state to undertake this operation. Despite the fact that the Allies were informed that no fresh troops were available and that the limits of resistance were rapidly approaching, no hope whatever of direct assistance from the French was forthcoming. That was the situation at the beginning of May 27th.

The last reserves, three weak regiments, were committed. Somehow or other we managed on our own to maintain contact with the British, but the enemy was determined to break down our resistance which was delaying him and causing him considerable losses. Our troops held along the whole of the front. They fought their ground, yielding only step by step under the repeated assaults of an enemy supported by an overwhelmingly large air force; they inflicted heavy losses on the enemy. The gunners emptied their ammunition limbers, firing point-blank and blowing up their guns when they were about to fall into the hands of the enemy. Despite such heroism, by about eleven o'clock large gaps were made on the front north of Maldegem, in the centre near Ursel, and to the right near Thielt and Roulers. The enemy advanced by infiltration. In the Thielt region, 6 to 7 km. of the front was left undefended; the enemy had only to pour through to reach Bruges. At about 12.30, the King telegraphed the following message to General Gort:

" The Belgian Army is losing heart. It has been fighting without a break for the past four days under a heavy bombardment which the R.A.F. has been unable to prevent. Having heard that the Allied group is surrounded and aware of the great superiority of the enemy, the troops have concluded that the situation is desperate. The time is rapidly

17153

approaching when they will be unable to continue the fight.
The King will be forced to capitulate to avoid a collapse."
At about 2.30 p.m. the French liaison authorities were
told that:
"Belgian resistance is at its last extremity; our front is
about to break like a worn bowstring."
The losses were heavy. The wounded were pouring into
the hospital units which were already overflowing; many
of the guns lacked ammunition. The Army could no longer
offer organized resistance. It had its back to the sea. The
arc of fire narrowed down; thousands of refugees and the
local population were wandering in a restricted area entirely
at the mercy of enemy guns and aircraft. More than 3
million people were crowded into less than 1,700 square km.
Many of them were homeless. Food was beginning to run
short. The Army no longer had access to a railway. The
roads were congested and traffic had great difficulty in
moving.
Our last means of resistance gave way under the crushing
weight of technical superiority. There was no hope of help
and no solution other than complete destruction. Shortly
before 4 p.m., the Belgian Command was forced to realize:
"(1) that from the national point of view, the Belgian Army
had carried out its task; it had resisted to the limit of its
capacity; its units were unable to continue the fight. There
could be no retreat to the Yser; it would do more to destroy
the units than the fighting in progress; it would increase
the congestion of the Allied forces to the highest pitch;
(2) from the international point of view, the despatch of an
envoy to ask for terms for the cessation of hostilities would
have the advantage of allowing the Allies the night of the
27th–28th and part of the morning of the 28th, an interval
that, if the fighting were continued, could be gained only
at the cost of the complete destruction of the Army." There
was no possibility of embarking; indeed, even if this solution
had been possible, it would have left uncovered the retreat
of the French and British forces to Dunkirk.
At 5 p.m. the King decided that an envoy should be sent

to the German Command to ask for an armistice between the Belgian Army and the German Army. This decision was at once communicated to the French and British Missions. The Head of the French Mission, while fully appreciating the justice of the decision, expressed the view that the negotiations should be conducted by the three armies in conjunction with one another. A little later a reply was given to the effect that the mission would confine itself to enquiring into the terms for the armistice. General Champon said, incidentally, that he had succeeded in getting into touch with General Weygand by wireless, but that he had been unable to reach General Blanchard, whose G.H.Q. was not where it was expected to be. He added that with our approval he would place on the Yser the 60th French Division which we had undertaken to send to Dunkirk in Belgian lorries so that it would come directly under French Command. Furthermore, he no longer knew where General Gort was to be found. His G.H.Q., which was to have established itself at Cassel, had had to give up this idea because of an attack by German tanks. Telephonic communication was impossible, because the Lille exchange had been destroyed.

At 5 p.m. Major-General Derousseaux, Deputy-Chief of the General Staff, left Belgian G.H.Q. He returned at 10 p.m. from G.H.Q. of the Eighteenth German Army with the reply: " The Führer demands that arms be laid down unconditionally " (Bedingungslos).

At 11 p.m., bowing to the inevitable, the King, in full agreement with his Chief of Staff, decided to accept the terms and proposed that firing should cease at 4 a.m.

May 28th.—At 1.30 a.m. the Head of the French Mission, who had moved, in the meantime, to La Panne, was informed of the capitulation.

At 4 a.m. firing ceased along the whole of the Belgian front, except in the Roulers–Ypres sector, where the Belgian units had not been informed of the capitulation and continued to defend their positions until about 6 a.m.

At about 9 a.m. a message from the envoy was received

to the effect that the German Command demanded free passage for its columns towards the sea. The message was at once telephoned to the Head of the French Mission. Shortly afterwards, communications between the representative of the Allied Command and the Belgian Command were finally severed by the breakdown of the telephone system.

The Protocol signed on May 28th by General von Reichenau for the German Army and General Derousseaux for the Belgian Army contained the following provisions :

" The Belgian Army shall unconditionally lay down its arms at once and shall from that time onwards regard itself as prisoner of war. An armistice was entered into this morning at 5 a.m.[1] at the request of the Belgian Command. The German operations against the British and French troops will not be suspended.

" Belgian territory will at once be occupied, including all the ports. No further damage shall be done to the locks or coastal fortifications.

" ADDITIONAL PROTOCOL

" 1. As a mark of honourable surrender, the Officers of the Belgian Army shall retain their weapons.

" 2. The Château of Laeken shall be placed at the disposal of His Majesty the King in order that he may reside there with his family, his military attendants and his servants."

This painful conclusion of an eighteen-day campaign was not unexpected. The British and French Government authorities were duly informed of our growing exhaustion and of our determination to defend our positions until all our means were expended : this was done. Capitulation was not the result of a free decision; it occurred, at the last extremity, under the inexorable pressure of events.

[1] German summer time.

Before parting with his Army, the King made a final proclamation:

"G.H.Q., *May 28th*, 1940.

"OFFICERS, NON-COMMISSIONED OFFICERS, AND MEN,

"Plunged unexpectedly into a war of unparalleled violence, you have fought courageously to defend your homeland step by step.

"Exhausted by an uninterrupted struggle against an enemy very much superior in numbers and in material, we have been forced to surrender.

"History will relate that the Army did its duty to the full. Our Honour is safe.

"This violent fighting, these sleepless nights, cannot have been in vain. I enjoin you not to be disheartened, but to bear yourselves with dignity. Let your attitude and your discipline continue to win you the esteem of the foreigner.

"I shall not leave you in our misfortune, and I shall watch over your future and that of your families.

"To-morrow we will set to work with the firm intention of raising our country from its ruins.

"LEOPOLD."

The Army had resisted the German aggression with all the means in its power. Its inability to check it was due to military events outside its control, events which occurred elsewhere. The Army had continued to fight desperately, despite the fact that it was irrevocably lost by the failure of the counter-attack to check the German envelopment. It did not lay down its arms until—with its back to the sea, hemmed in to the last remaining strip of territory, and with no means of escape—it could continue the struggle no longer. As he had proclaimed in order to strengthen the courage of his soldiers at the height of the battle, its Commander-in-Chief has since linked up his future with that of the Army. By his dignified attitude, in the captivity to which he has condemned himself, by his refusal to recognize the accomplished fact, he has shown himself to be the incarnation of a people which will not accept servitude.

Appendix 1

SPEECH BY THE KING TO THE COUNCIL OF MINISTERS ON OCTOBER 14TH, 1936

GENTLEMEN,

In taking the constitutional oath, Belgian sovereigns undertake to maintain the integrity and independence of their country. I, like my predecessors, intend to keep this solemn promise. That is why I was anxious to preside over this Council which is to draw up measures for submission to Parliament for the purpose of providing Belgium with a military status adapted to the present circumstances.

For over a year already, the Government has been considering how we can strengthen our present military position.

There were several reasons for this :

(*a*) German rearmament, following upon the complete remilitarization of Italy and Russia, caused most other States, even those that were deliberately pacific, like Switzerland and the Netherlands, to take exceptional precautions.

(*b*) There has been such a vast change in methods of warfare as a result of technical progress, particularly in aviation and mechanization, that the initial operations of an armed conflict can now be of such force, speed, and magnitude as to be particularly alarming to small countries like Belgium.

(*c*) Our anxieties have been increased by the lightning reoccupation of the Rhineland and the fact that bases for the start of a possible German invasion have been moved near to our frontier.

(*d*) At the same time, the foundations of international security have been shaken because conventions, even conventions freely subscribed to, have been violated, and in the present circumstances it is almost impossible to adapt the Covenant of the League of Nations so as to prevent such violations.

(*e*) Lastly, there is a danger that the internal dissensions in certain States may lead other States to be embroiled in rivalry between different political and social systems and may let loose a fiercer and more devastating conflagration than that from the after-effects of which we are still suffering.

It might perhaps be as well to recall here the successive stages through which the examination of the military problem has passed during the last few months.

This summary will also show that the series of studies has now been completed.

The need for adjusting our military forces to meet external risks and dangers became apparent in the spring of 1935. The Army General Staff placed various schemes before me, and finally, in November 1935, I approved of a programme the main principles of which seemed to me to constitute a minimum.

This programme was submitted to the Government, which formed a small committee to make a thorough investigation of the problem of security.

On February 7th, 1936, the Cabinet Council agreed upon the text of a draft military law; this did not meet with the approval of all sections of the Chamber, and the Government agreed to the tabling of an amendment providing for the immediate application of Article 53 of the Militia Law. The Bill as amended was passed by the Chamber on April 6th.

Meanwhile, it was suggested on January 10th that the whole problem should be discussed by a mixed commission.

This idea was welcomed in political and parliamentary circles.

The mixed commission was set up by Royal Decree on March 25th, 1936.

After thirty-seven meetings, during which every aspect of the problem was discussed, the commission completed its work and reached a number of conclusions. While there is some difference of opinion as to their application, there is unanimity on general principles, particularly on the need for a permanent covering force. The main suggestions—purchases of material, anti-aircraft defence, fortification, the calling-up system—call for an immediate decision.

In any event, the new Militia Law must be passed before December 1st, as the call-up of the 1937 class begins on that date.

Furthermore, in view of the dangerous international situation, the country will expect the Government to submit the necessary proposals to Parliament without delay. Again, the precise nature of the problem should be explained to the public.

Our military policy, like our foreign policy, on which it depends, must aim, not at preparing for a more or less successful war, following upon a coalition, but at keeping war from our territory.

The reoccupation of the Rhineland strained the Locarno agreements in both the letter and the spirit, and we are now in almost the same international situation as before the war.

Because of our geographical situation we need a military machine large enough to dissuade any of our neighbours from making use of our territory to attack another State. By the discharge of this mission, we make a valuable contribution towards peace in Western Europe; and *ipso facto* it gives us a right to the respect, and if necessary to the help, of all the States that are interested in peace.

I believe Belgian opinion is unanimous as to these principles. But our undertakings should not go beyond that. A unilateral policy would weaken our position abroad and rightly or wrongly would cause dissension at home. An alliance, even if it were purely defensive, would not lead to the desired object; for however promptly an ally might come to our aid, the impact of the invasion—and it would be overwhelming—would come first, and we should have to meet it by ourselves.

In the absence of a defence system of her own, capable of withstanding the invader, the invasion would penetrate deeply into Belgium at the very beginning and she would be devastated at once. Afterwards friendly intervention might, of course, ensure final victory, but in the process the country would suffer ravages such as would be infinitely worse than those of the war of 1914–18.

That is why our policy must be " solely and exclusively Belgian," as the Minister for Foreign Affairs said recently. Its resolute aim must be to keep us out of the conflicts of our neighbours; it is in keeping with our national ideals. It can be maintained by a reasonable military and financial effort, and it will be welcomed by Belgians, all inspired by an intense and primordial desire for peace.

Let any who doubt whether such a foreign policy is possible consider the proud and confident example set by Holland and Switzerland.

Let them remember how much Belgium's scrupulous observance of her neutrality weighed in our favour and in favour of the Allies during the whole of the war and the subsequent settlement.

Morally our position would have been incomparably weaker at home, and the world would not have shown us so much sympathy if the invader had been able to point to an alliance between ourselves and one of his opponents.

It is therefore, I repeat, solely at preserving ourselves from war, wherever it may threaten, that our military system must aim; and it is important that public opinion should be absolutely certain of this.

Our military status, which derives from the 1929 Militia Law, though excellent in various respects, is no longer suitable, having regard to the new possibility of a sudden invasion. It secures neither the permanent defence of our frontiers, nor safety to mobilize, nor the concentration of the Army. A more or less unexpected irruption might, in a few hours, seize valuable sureties and paralyse irrevocably the greater part of our forces.

This defective machinery is in urgent need of repair. I have

5

called you together so that we may decide how this shall be done.

As representatives of the three great traditional Parties, who speak for the vast majority of Belgians, I hope you will approve the Bill of the Minister of National Defence.

If you can unite in a spirit of high patriotic understanding to solve the military problem, you will at the same time restore to the country the necessary serenity of mind in the face of outward events and the atmosphere of security essential to general prosperity.

Thus you will once again prove to the country that the chief preoccupation of the National Coalition Government is to put the higher interests of Belgium above everything else.

Appendix 2

FRANCO-BRITISH DECLARATION OF APRIL 24TH, 1937[1]

IN accordance with instructions received from their respective Governments, His Majesty's Ambassador and the French Ambassador have the honour to make the following communication to the Belgian Government :

1. The Governments of the United Kingdom of Great Britain and Northern Ireland and of the French Republic have not failed during the last few months to give their full attention to the desire of the Belgian Government to have the international rights and obligations of Belgium clarified in certain respects where this is rendered necessary by her geographical position and by the delays which may still occur before the negotiation and conclusion of the general Act intended to replace the Treaty of Lausanne.

2. The Government of the United Kingdom and the Government of the Republic, being anxious to give full expression to their sympathy with this desire of the Belgian Government, have agreed to make the following declaration:

3. The said Governments have taken note of the views which the Belgian Government has itself expressed concerning the interests of Belgium, and more particularly—

(1) The determination expressed publicly and on more than one occasion by the Belgian Government: (*a*) to defend the frontiers of Belgium with all its forces against any aggression or invasion, and to prevent Belgian territory

[1] British White Paper, Cmd. 5437.

from being used, for purposes of aggression against another State, as a passage or as a base of operations by land, by sea, or in the air; (*b*) to organize the defence of Belgium in an efficient manner for this purpose;

(2) The renewed assurances of the fidelity of Belgium to the Covenant of the League of Nations and to the obligations which it involves for Members of the League.

4. In consequence, taking into account the determination and assurances mentioned above, the Government of the United Kingdom and the Government of the Republic declare that they consider Belgium to be now released from all obligations towards them resulting from either the Treaty of Locarno or the arrangements drawn up in London on March 19th, 1936, and that they maintain in respect of Belgium the undertakings of assistance which they entered into towards her under the above-mentioned instruments.

5. The Government of the United Kingdom and the Government of the Republic agree that the release of Belgium from her obligations, as provided for in paragraph 4 above, in no way affects the existing undertakings between the United Kingdom and France.

ACKNOWLEDGMENT OF RECEIPT[1]

The Royal Government has taken note with great satisfaction of the declaration communicated to it this day by the Government of the United Kingdom of Great Britain and Northern Ireland. It thanks the Government of the United Kingdom warmly for this communication.

Appendix 3

SPEECH IN THE CHAMBER OF REPRESENTATIVES BY M. SPAAK, MINISTER FOR FOREIGN AFFAIRS, ON APRIL 29TH, 1937

COMMUNICATION FROM THE GOVERNMENT

M. SPAAK, *Minister for Foreign Affairs and Foreign Trade.*— Last Saturday M. Laroche, Ambassador of France, and Sir Esmond Ovey, Ambassador of Great Britain, handed me the Franco-British Declaration which you will no doubt have read in the newspapers.

I should like, however, to remind you of it, for I want you to

[1] British White Paper, Cmd. 5437.

have its terms in your minds while I am speaking. It reads as follows:

" In accordance with instructions received from their respective Governments, His Majesty's Ambassador and the French Ambassador have the honour to make the following communication to the Belgian Government:

" 1. The Governments of the United Kingdom of Great Britain and Northern Ireland and of the French Republic have not failed during the last few months to give their full attention to the desire of the Belgian Government to have the international rights and obligations of Belgium clarified in certain respects where this is rendered necessary by her geographical position and by the delays which may still occur before the negotiation and conclusion of the general Act intended to replace the Treaty of Lausanne.

" 2. The Government of the United Kingdom and the Government of the Republic, being anxious to give full expression to their sympathy with this desire of the Belgian Government, have agreed to make the following declaration:

" 3. The said Governments have taken note of the views which the Belgian Government has itself expressed concerning the interests of Belgium, and more particularly—

" (1) The determination expressed publicly and on more than one occasion by the Belgian Government: (a) to defend the frontiers of Belgium with all its forces against any aggression or invasion, and to prevent Belgian territory from being used, for purposes of aggression against another State, as a passage or as a base of operations by land, by sea, or in the air; (b) to organize the defence of Belgium in an efficient manner for this purpose;

" (2) The renewed assurances of the fidelity of Belgium to the Covenant of the League of Nations and to the obligations which it involves for Members of the League.

" 4. In consequence, taking into account the determination and assurances mentioned above, the Government of the United Kingdom and the Government of the Republic declare that they consider Belgium to be now released from all obligations towards them resulting from either the Treaty of Locarno or the arrangements drawn up in London on March 19th, 1936, and that they maintain in respect of Belgium the undertakings of assistance which they entered into towards her under the above-mentioned instruments." (Hear, hear !)

" 5. The Government of the United Kingdom and the Govern-
of the Republic agree that the release of Belgium from her
obligations, as provided for in paragraph 4 above, in no way
affects the existing undertakings between the United Kingdom
and France."

I handed the two Ambassadors the following reply on behalf
of the Government:

" BRUSSELS, *April* 24*th*, 1937.

" YOUR EXCELLENCY,
" The Royal Government has taken note with great
satisfaction of the declaration communicated to it this day by
the Government of the United Kingdom of Great Britain and
Northern Ireland. It thanks the Government of the United
Kingdom warmly for this communication.
" I have the honour, etc." (More signs of approval.)

I think it only right to add to my own expression of satisfaction
the expression of Belgium's gratitude. For some months I have
found in British and French statesmen—Mr. Eden as well as
M. Blum and M. Delbos—and also M. Laroche and Sir Esmond
Ovey, for I must not forget these good servants of their own
countries who are also great friends of ours—the most loyal and
complete spirit of understanding and collaboration. (Hear,
hear!)

Mr. Eden said the other day at Brussels:
" Every country has different problems to face. Every
country has its own internal troubles; every country has special
difficulties for which a special solution is necessary. In these
circumstances, we must—each in so far as we are concerned—
make allowances if we are to make any progress."

How could we fail to arrive at a solution when the statesman
with whom we discuss our problems is inspired by such concilia-
tory wisdom ?

M. Blum and M. Delbos showed no less foresight, and what
has happened in the last few days is therefore really the result
of understanding and mutual confidence between France, Great
Britain, and Belgium.

I should like to tell you all once more in public—you who
represent the nation—that while it is true that we have been
released by our great neighbours from certain legal obligations,
they have acquired a new title to our friendship and gratitude.
(Loud applause.)

Six days ago, then, an important change was made in our
international status.

The first question we must answer is this: Were there any

reasons why we should try to define and specify our international rights and duties in a new form ? I do not think there can be the slightest doubt as to the importance, the absolute necessity, of doing so.

To be sure of this we have only to remind ourselves of what our status was before. We have only to compare the period when it was thought out with to-day.

Belgium was happy to sign the Treaty of Locarno, and I sincerely believe she was right to sign it, for she obtained something that was essential to her security—the guarantee of France, Great Britain, and Italy.

However, the Treaty of Locarno imposed on us certain obligations which, though we were able to support them ten years ago, now seem to be far too onerous.

By the Treaty of Locarno, Belgium guaranteed to maintain the territorial *status quo* arising out of the frontiers between Germany and France and also the inviolability of those frontiers.

Thus, Belgium guaranteed France against a possible German attack; but—and many Belgians seem to have forgotten this—she also guaranteed Germany against a possible French attack.

By the Treaty of Locarno, despite the fundamental differences in our situation and in our available resources, we adopted exactly the same attitude and obligations in Western Europe as did our greater neighbours.

That was unquestionably daring. It is true that the atmosphere in Europe, as well as certain special circumstances, were such as to explain and justify our boldness.

The Germany of that time was almost disarmed, and there was reason to hope that the world would be wise enough to seek salvation in concerted and controlled disarmament. That hope is to-day disappointed—temporarily, I hope—but truth compels us to admit that Germany has again become a great military nation, and that in all countries throughout the world the armaments race has begun again with an intensity never before equalled.

That is the first fundamental difference between 1920 and 1937.

In 1925, there was a demilitarized zone. Articles 42 and 43 of the Treaty of Versailles were still effective. Article 1 of the Treaty of Locarno referred specifically to them. There is no need for me to emphasize the importance of the demilitarized zone for our military security in the event of a German attack.

In 1936, Germany reoccupied the demilitarized zone, reversing the former situation and facing us with a new fact.

How could we fail to take account of it in formulating our international status ?

Lastly, in 1925 Germany was preparing to enter the League of Nations, and we were preparing to welcome her, knowing full well that her presence at Geneva would enhance the League's prestige and make it more effective.

Germany was ready in 1925 to accept the obligations and duties to which we subscribed when we adhered to the Covenant; her policy was to be based on the same principles as ours, and that was an important factor in our security.

Germany has now left the League; unfortunately, the hour for her return has not come yet. This fact must also be taken into account.

This simple reminder of the past, this simple comparison between 1925 and 1937, brings out the difference between the problems facing us to-day and the problems that faced us twelve years ago. It explains why different solutions are justified.

The story would, however, be incomplete if I omitted the events of March 7th, 1936. In reoccupying the demilitarized zone, in repudiating the Treaty of Locarno, Germany placed France, Great Britain, Italy, and Belgium in a difficult situation.

In London, the three countries most directly concerned sought means of meeting the situation. They made arrangements which they themselves regarded as provisional. Above all—and I think I may pay them this tribute—they never lost heart, in spite of their very understandable bitterness and disappointment. They set to work again without losing hope, but with the determination to aim at peace, whatever happened.

They resumed their negotiations; they reformulated their proposals; they tried once again to create confidence and a spirit of understanding.

The work they had undertaken was long and exacting; it was arduous; it required time. I still firmly hope that one day it will be successful.

Yet the provisional system adopted in London was particularly burdensome for a small country. France and Great Britain quite understood this; they both felt, with us, that the agreement reached in March 1936 to meet a new situation that had arisen unexpectedly should be reviewed and readjusted.

Belgium was legitimately anxious to return at once to a more normal international status, a status better adapted to her resources and traditions.

The Prime Minister and I have often tried to explain these ideas. The King gave new force to them in his speech of October 14th, and public opinion has almost unanimously approved of them.

What are the principles on which our foreign policy is based ?
I should like to remind you of them again.   We want first and
foremost to find a formula for uniting our people.   We do not
want to make sacrifices for the sake of a specifically Walloon or
specifically Flemish ideology.   We want a policy that is solely
and exclusively Belgian.   We want a policy firmly rooted in our
national traditions, a policy which will help us to play our part in
Europe.

Belgium has no direct interests outside her own frontiers; she
has no ambition other than to remain what she is; she seeks
nothing; she asks nothing of anyone but peace.   (Hear, hear !)

But—and this is both her misfortune and her greatness—she
has for centuries been a European battlefield, a highway for
invasion for all the conquerors.   Her rôle, the rôle entrusted
to her, one she must fulfil, is to close up on all sides and in all
directions the way of invasion; to erect so many barriers and
create so many difficulties on the battlefield of Europe that even
the boldest are deterred.

That is why our military policy is so closely bound up with our
foreign policy.   If Europe has more confidence in us to-day, it is
not only because of our loyal attitude.   It is because a few
months ago, for the first time in our history, we all together
shouldered the heavy burdens demanded of us.

But apart from this we also want to contribute towards the
collective organization of peace, towards the formulation of an
international law.   In spite of failure, in spite of disillusionment,
we should like to feel that one day wisdom and reason will prevail.
That is why we are faithful to the League of Nations and why we
offer it our loyal collaboration.

All this we have said over and over again.   France and Great
Britain heard and understood; in their joint declaration they
defined our foreign policy in terms not a single word of which do
I need to alter:

" The said Governments have taken note of the views which the
Belgian Government has itself expressed concerning the interests
of Belgium, and more particularly—

> " (1) The determination expressed publicly and on more than
> one occasion by the Belgian Government: (*a*) to defend
> the frontiers of Belgium with all its forces against any
> aggression or invasion, and to prevent Belgian territory
> from being used, for purposes of aggression against
> another State, as a passage or as a base of operations
> by land, by sea, or in the air; (*b*) to organize the defence
> of Belgium in an efficient manner for this purpose;

" (2) The renewed assurances of the fidelity of Belgium to the Covenant of the League of Nations and to the obligations which it involves for Members of the League."

Having thus defined our foreign policy, France and Great Britain of their own accord took a twofold decision. They released us from the guarantees we had given them in Locarno and London, and they maintained the guarantees they had given us.

That is our new position. I very sincerely believe that it represents an improvement on which we can congratulate ourselves.

Why an improvement? Because it is simple; because it is clear; because we now know exactly what our obligations are; because from now on there is only one ground on which we can be forced to make war: one ground about which there can be no discussion, no controversy; one ground about which we should all be united and resolute—the defence of our territory against an enemy attack. (Hear, hear !)

The declaration of April 24th is not a treaty in the strict sense. It is a spontaneous act on the part of France and Great Britain, but it is justified by the definition of our foreign policy. It follows that if one day we use our freedom to modify our policy, France and Great Britain will be entitled to withdraw their guarantee.

There can be no doubt as to these principles.

I therefore sincerely believe that everyone will admit that we are in a stronger position to-day than we were before, since, while we are released from some of our obligations, we retain all our rights.

But this brings me to the possible objection of those who feel we are being selfish, those who, in the language of international law, affirm that we have failed to be loyal to the principles of collective security and mutual assistance.

Frankly I do not agree. But if we are to make ourselves heard and understood, we must break down the barrier, tear away the screen of language, and get at the facts.

If collective security is a notion that implies that all States, whatever their size, whatever their strength or their traditions or their geographical situation, must adopt the same attitude, must subscribe to the same undertakings, if it means that Belgium's policy must be identical with the policy of France, Great Britain, or Germany, then I say collective security is a vague ideology which can never be of any service, for it is deeply opposed to the facts and possibilities. (Hear, hear !) But if collective security means that to promote the common welfare of all peoples, the organization and maintenance of peace, each State must do its utmost to play its part in so far as its resources permit, then I agree, and I would add that that is Belgium's position. For what is important is not what undertakings we give, but what undertakings we keep. And I repeat once more that in organizing our national defences, in making a great military effort, in not quibbling about what form aggression against us may take, in facing the cruel risks that all this entails, Belgium is giving Europe everything she can give, everything that Europe can legitimately ask of her. (Hear, hear!)

That, then, is how Great Britain and France and Belgium have settled for themselves the obligations of the past.

There remains the future.

The efforts begun during the past few months will continue. The Franco-British Declaration makes this clear. In particular, an immediate solution was sought and found for certain problems, seeing that the negotiations for a Western pact may take some time.

Belgium intends to take part in these negotiations. The Government is well aware that the work will not be completed until formulas have been found that are acceptable to Germany.

I have already explained how much importance I attach to the last declaration of the Chancellor of the German Reich. It testified to a state of mind which we cannot but approve; it suggests possibilities which I have no intention of abandoning. The difficulties are not insurmountable. The state of mind with which we approach them is a fundamental factor in success or failure. The state of Europe is better to-day than it was six months ago, and the Franco-British Declaration is a new factor making for appeasement.

It is a fact that most European statesmen have a good-will towards peace, and we must have confidence.

We have passed the first stage. I envisage the stage we are now approaching with optimism. That is all I need say about the Franco-British Declaration.

There remain two problems which are not dealt with in the declaration. But I should like to say a few words about them, for I know Belgian public opinion and European public opinion are interested. I refer to the interpretation of Article 16 of the Covenant and to what is known as the question of General Staff agreements.

I shall have very little to say about Article 16, for I think it is for the Assembly at Geneva to give an official interpretation of the texts. But in view of the present discussions, the Chamber will expect me to express some opinion on it.

Moreover, I hope what I am going to say will help to clear up a problem which will only become more confused and difficult to solve if we are unduly cautious and subtle.

Here I am following the example of M. de Graeff, the honourable Minister for Foreign Affairs of the Netherlands, who has just made important and noteworthy declarations in the Netherlands Parliament.

The most important and most difficult part of Article 16 is the paragraph before the last dealing with the right of passage: The Members of the League of Nations " will take the necessary steps to afford passage through their territory to the forces of any of the Members of the League which are co-operating to protect the covenants of the League."

How and when would this operate?

It is quite extraordinary—and I might almost say disquieting— that so important a text, the application of which may produce serious consequences, should still be left open to individual interpretation.

As far as the Belgian Government is concerned, there are two conditions fundamental to affording the right of passage through our territory. The first is that on no hypothesis could passage be afforded without the consent of Belgium. The second is that Belgium could only give her consent in the case of joint action.

There does not seem to me to be any serious doubt as to these two conditions.

The first is the only possible interpretation compatible with our full sovereignty, the only interpretation compatible also with our public law.

This is so obvious that I do not need to demonstrate it.

The second condition—that there must be joint action—follows from the text itself.

I would not, of course, go so far as to maintain that joint action means the effective participation of all the Members of the League of Nations without exception; but it does mean, if we are to be reasonably satisfied, that our neighbours must participate.

Those are the main ideas I hope to defend at Geneva when the question is raised there. (Hear, hear!)

In so far as General Staff agreements are concerned, my reply will be clear. The Franco-British Declaration of April 24th closes for us the period that might be described as the era of military agreements, and I am glad of it. (Hear, hear!)

Here some explanation is called for.

I am glad of it, not because these agreements were bad, but

because in spite of the facts, in spite of affirmations ten times, twenty times, repeated by all my predecessors, they lent themselves, both at home and in Europe, to confusion and mistrust.

To some of us they were proof of our enfeoffment to one of our great neighbours. Others regarded them as an essential factor in our national defence. Each view was as false as the other.

Now these military agreements are done away with, I solemnly repeat again that they were not political; that they in no way impaired our independence; and that the spirit in which they were conceived was always the spirit in which they were applied.

That being so, where are we now?

The merit of the Franco-British Declaration, as I have said already—and I now repeat it—is to have clarified the situation. For us to-day there is only one possible ground for war—national defence.

The military problems of our responsible authorities are therefore now freed of any superfluous complications due to our responsibility for guarantees.

The problem is simplified—it is a purely technical problem.

Our foreign policy is now in line with what we can do in the military sphere.

We are free to deal quite independently with the technical problem; we have not agreed, and we shall never agree, to the slightest interference, the smallest restriction.

Once again we give a formal undertaking: whatever we ought to do to ensure the national defence, within the lines laid down above, will be done.

That is the end of this unduly lengthy declaration. I have nothing of importance to add to it.

The Government of national coalition and renewal has set itself the task, with the support of your confident co-operation, of making Belgium more prosperous, more socially developed, and more strong.

It is convinced that in attaining to the stage of foreign policy I have just described, it has made a useful contribution to that end.

It awaits and expects your approval. Your approval will crown its efforts, and once again the world will have the spectacle of a free people, magnificently confident of the destiny of the Fatherland. (Loud applause.)

Appendix 4

GERMAN DECLARATION OF OCTOBER 13TH, 1937

MONSIEUR LE MINISTRE,

I have the honour, on behalf of the German Government, to make the following communication to your Excellency:

The German Government has taken cognizance, with particular interest, of the public declarations in which the Belgian Government defines the international position of Belgium. For its part, it has repeatedly given expression, especially through the declaration of the Chancellor of the German Reich in his speech of January 30th, 1937, to its own point of view.

The German Government has also taken cognizance of the declaration made by the British and French Governments on April 24th, 1937.

Since the conclusion of a treaty to replace the Treaty of Locarno may still take some time, and being desirous of strengthening the peaceful aspirations of the two countries, the German Government regards it as appropriate to define now its own attitude towards Belgium.

To this end it makes the following declaration:

(1) The German Government has taken note of the views which the Belgian Government has thought fit to express; that is to say:

(*a*) Of the policy of independence which it intends to exercise in full sovereignty;

(*b*) Of its determination to defend the frontiers of Belgium with all its forces against any aggression or invasion, and to prevent Belgian territory from being used, for purposes of aggression against another State, as a passage or as a base of operations by land, by sea, or in the air; and to organize the defence of Belgium in an efficient manner for this purpose.

(2) The German Government considers that the inviolability and integrity of Belgium are common interests of the Western Powers. It confirms its determination that in no circumstances will it impair this inviolability and integrity, and that it will at all times respect Belgian territory, except, of course, in the event of Belgium's taking part in a military action directed against Germany in an armed conflict in which Germany is involved.

(3) The German Government, like the British and French Governments, is prepared to assist Belgium should she be subjected to an attack or to invasion.

I have the honour, etc.

ACKNOWLEDGMENT OF RECEIPT

The Belgian Government has taken note with great satisfaction of the declaration communicated to it this day by the German Government. It thanks the German Government warmly for this communication.

Appendix 5

DECLARATION MADE BY KING LEOPOLD ON BEHALF OF THE HEADS OF THE STATES OF THE OSLO GROUP, AUGUST 23RD, 1939

THE declaration I am about to read is made at the Palace of Brussels before the Ministers for Foreign Affairs and on behalf of the Heads of the States of the Oslo Group.

The world is passing through a period of tension which threatens to put a stop to all normal collaboration between States. Great Powers take measures that amount almost to the mobilization of their armed forces. Have not the small Powers good reason to fear that they may become the victims of a conflict into which they might be drawn against their wills? Although they have indubitably followed a policy of independence and have made no secret of their strong determination to remain neutral, are they not open to the danger of being affected by arrangements made without their knowledge?

Even in the absence of hostilities, the world is threatened with economic collapse. Distrust and suspicion are everywhere. Under our very eyes the factions are gathering; the armies are forming; a terrifying struggle is about to begin in Europe. Shall our Continent destroy itself in a fearful war in which there will be neither victor nor vanquished, a conflict that will engulf the spiritual and material values built up through centuries of civilization?

The war psychosis is invading our own lands, and public opinion, though well aware of what an unthinkable disaster a conflagration would constitute for the whole of mankind, is increasingly giving way to the idea that we must inevitably be drawn into it. We must counteract this fatal mood of resignation.

Not a single people—we are absolutely convinced—would willingly send its children to their death in order to deprive other nations of their right of existence.

States have, of course, different interests. But are there any interests that cannot be reconciled with one another more easily before than after a war ?

Let the conscience of the world be roused! The worst may still be avoided, but time presses. The course of events may very soon render any direct contact between us even more difficult.

Let there be no mistake ! We know that the right to live must be founded on a firm basis, and the peace that we want is peace with respect for the rights of all nations. A durable peace cannot be based on force. It can only be based on a moral order.

Does not wisdom command us to make a truce of this war of words, of provocations and threats, to be ready to discuss our problems with one another ? We solemnly urge those who hold the future in their hands to agree to submit their disputes and their claims to open negotiation in a spirit of brotherly co-operation.

For that reason, on behalf of:

His Majesty the King of Denmark,
The President of the Republic of Finland,
Her Royal Highness the Grand Duchess of Luxemburg,
His Majesty the King of Norway,
Her Majesty the Queen of the Netherlands,
His Majesty the King of Sweden,

and on my own behalf, each of us acting with the approval of our Governments, I make this appeal. We hope that other Heads of States may show the same solicitude for the peace and security of their peoples and may join their appeal to ours.

To-morrow hundreds of millions will welcome our plea that the course of the war be arrested. May those who hold the future of the world in their hands show themselves responsive to these sentiments and see that their often-expressed desire to settle their differences by peaceful means is achieved.

And may the disaster which threatens mankind be averted!

Appendix 6

DECLARATION MADE BY THE AMBASSADOR OF GERMANY ON AUGUST 26TH, 1939

IN view of the gravity of the international situation, I am expressly instructed by the Head of the German Reich to transmit to Your Majesty the following communication:

Though the German Government is at present doing everything in its power to arrive at a peaceful solution of the questions at issue between the Reich and Poland, it nevertheless desires to define clearly, here and now, the attitude which it proposes to adopt towards Belgium should a conflict in Europe become inevitable.

The German Government is firmly determined to abide by the terms of the Declaration contained in the German Note of October 13th, 1937. This provides, in effect, that Germany will in no circumstances impair the inviolability and integrity of Belgium and will at all times respect Belgian territory. The German Government renews this undertaking, however, in the expectation that the Belgian Government, for its part, will observe an attitude of strict neutrality and that Belgium will tolerate no violation on the part of a third Power, but that on the contrary she will oppose it with all the force at her disposal. It goes without saying that if the Belgian Government were to adopt a different attitude, the German Government would naturally be compelled to defend its interests in conformity with the new situation thus created.

Appendix 7

DECLARATION MADE BY THE AMBASSADOR OF GREAT BRITAIN ON AUGUST 27TH, 1939

HIS Majesty's Government in the United Kingdom have neglected no steps which might contribute to the maintenance of peace. Should these efforts fail, they know that Belgium will scrupulously abide by her international obligations. If Belgium adopts an attitude of neutrality, His Majesty's Government will, in accordance with their traditional policy, be resolute and determined to respect this neutrality fully. Only in the event of Belgian neutrality not being respected by other powers would the United Kingdom be led to modify its attitude in order to ensure its own defence. The undertakings of assistance which the United Kingdom has entered into towards Belgium, and which were expressly maintained in the communication to the Belgian Government of April 24th, 1937, naturally retain their full effect.

DECLARATION MADE BY THE AMBASSADOR OF FRANCE ON AUGUST 28TH, 1939

FRENCH EMBASSY IN BELGIUM,
BRUSSELS, *August 28th*, 1939.

THE Government of the Republic have neglected no steps which might contribute to the maintenance of peace. Should these

AMBASSADE DE FRANCE
EN BELGIQUE

BRUXELLES.LE 28 Août 1939.

Le Gouvernement de la République n'a rien négligé
de ce qui peut contribuer au maintien de la paix. Si ses
efforts venaient à échouer, il sait que le Gouvernement
Belge saurait se conformer exactement à ses obligations
internationales.

Dans le cas où la Belgique adopterait une position
de neutralité, le Gouvernement Français resterait, bien
entendu, comme en 1914, résolu à respecter pleinement cette
neutralité. Ce n'est qu'au cas où la neutralité Belge ne
serait pas respectée par une autre Puissance que la France,
pour assurer sa propre défense, pourrait être amenée à mo-
difier son attitude.

Les engagements d'assistance que le Gouvernement
français a pris envers la Belgique et qui ont été expres-
sément maintenus dans sa communication au Gouvernement
belge du 24 Avril 1937 conservent naturellement leur plei-
ne valeur./.

COPY OF A DECLARATION MADE BY THE FRENCH AMBASSADOR,
AUGUST 28TH, 1939

efforts fail, they know that Belgium will scrupulously abide by her international obligations. If Belgium adopts an attitude of neutrality, the French Government will, of course, as in 1914, be resolute to respect this neutrality fully. Only in the event of Belgian neutrality not being respected by another power would France be led to modify its attitude in order to ensure its own defence. The undertakings of assistance which the French Government has entered into towards Belgium, and which were expressly maintained in the communication to the Belgian Government of April 24th, 1937, naturally retain their full effect.

Appendix 8

DECLARATION OF NEUTRALITY
September 3rd, 1939

THE Belgian Government declares that it is firmly determined to maintain its neutrality in the conflict which has just broken out in Europe. Consequently, the following rules will immediately be put into operation:

I

No hostile act shall be permitted and no base for hostile operations shall be established within the limits of the jurisdiction of the State, including the territory of the Kingdom in Europe and the Colonies and Possessions under mandate, the territorial sea and the air space over such territory and territorial sea.

Territorial sea shall be understood to mean the sea round the coast to a breadth of three nautical miles, at the rate of 60 per degree of latitude, measured from the low-water line.

II

It shall not be permitted:

1. For any part of the territory whatsoever to be occupied by a belligerent military force;

2. For troops or convoys of munitions or war supplies to enter or pass through this territory by land;

3. For belligerent warships or similar vessels to enter or pass through the territorial sea;

4. For belligerent military aircraft or similar aircraft to enter or traverse the territory, territorial sea or air space over such territory or territorial sea within the jurisdiction of the State.

III

Merchant vessels armed for defence may enter and remain in ports and roadsteads after complying with the prescriptions enacted by the local authorities in the interests of security. The number of such vessels in each port or roadstead, however, may not exceed the maximum laid down by the local authorities in the interests of the security of the country.

Vessels carrying not more than two guns of a calibre of over 8 cm. and under 16 cm. and a crew not appreciably larger in effectives than is required for commercial operations shall be regarded as armed for defence.

IV

Troops or soldiers forming part of a belligerent force who may come within the jurisdiction of the State shall be disarmed and interned.

Warships or similar vessels belonging to the belligerents which shall infringe the provisions of Article 2 or Article 7 shall be seized, and their crews and any military passengers shall be interned.

Military aircraft or similar aircraft belonging to the belligerents which shall enter the jurisdiction of the State shall be seized and their crews shall be interned. Such aircraft shall be forced to land or to alight should they fail to do so of their own accord.

Aircraft on board a warship or similar vessel shall be deemed to form part of the latter, provided that while the vessel remains within the jurisdiction of the State they remain on board.

V

Notwithstanding Article 4, the following shall not be interned:

(*a*) Shipwrecked persons, or persons who are sick or wounded, provided they have not taken part in hostile acts within the jurisdiction of the State;

(*b*) Soldiers on board a merchant vessel not ranking as a warship, which is merely calling at a port or roadstead;

(*c*) Escaped prisoners of war;

(*d*) Deserters.

VI

The provisions of Articles 2 and 4 shall not apply to:

(1) A belligerent warship or other similar vessel which is able to prove that by reason of damage sustained or the condition of

the sea, it is compelled to enter a port or roadstead of the State, provided that it shall not be pursued by the enemy.

A vessel may only repair damage in so far as this is essential to safe navigation, and it may not in any manner whatsoever increase its military strength.

It shall leave the said port or roadstead as soon as the circumstances which caused it to take refuge there shall have ceased to exist. The Government may fix a time-limit after which the vessel may be seized and the crew and military passengers interned. Members of the crew and military passengers who remain on land after the vessel has left shall be interned.

(2) Warships and similar vessels which are able to prove that they entered the jurisdiction of the State owing to *force majeure* and in spite of having taken every precautionary measure to avoid it.

(3) Warships, aircraft, or similar vessels and machines which are employed solely for religious, scientific, or philanthropic missions.

VII

A belligerent warship or similar vessel which may find itself in a port or roadstead, or even in territorial waters, when war breaks out, shall leave within a time-limit laid down by the local authorities.

Belligerent aircraft or similar aircraft within the jurisdiction of the State on the publication of the Declaration of Neutrality shall be interned.

VIII

In the cases provided for under Articles 6 and 7, if warships or similar vessels belonging to the two belligerent parties should find themselves simultaneously in close proximity to one another, at least twenty-four hours shall elapse between the departure of the vessel of one belligerent and the departure of the vessel of the other belligerent.

Vessels shall leave in the order in which they arrived, except in special circumstances.

A belligerent warship may not leave a port or roadstead until at least twenty-four hours after the departure of a merchant vessel flying the flag of its enemy.

IX

Warships or similar vessels covered by Article 7 shall only be permitted to revictual in ports and roadsteads for the purpose of replenishing their normal peace-time stores of food and water.

Similarly, such vessels may only take on fuel to enable them to reach the nearest port in their own or allied country.

Warships or similar vessels covered by Article 6 (1) may replenish their stores of food, water, and fuel in so far as this is necessary for their requirements during their stay.

X

Prizes may not be taken into waters subject to the jurisdiction of the State.

Should a prize be taken into the said waters, it shall be released, together with its crew.

The crew placed on board by the captor shall be interned, provided that the prize was not brought in owing to damage or to the bad condition of the sea.

XI

Any war material washed ashore or found in the sea and subsequently brought to land shall be seized unless it is necessary to destroy it in the interests of public safety.

XII

Combatant corps may not be formed or enlistment offices opened in the territory of the State for the benefit of the belligerents.

XIII

It shall be prohibited, within the jurisdiction of the State, to take service on board belligerent warships or similar vessels.

It shall be prohibited, within the jurisdiction of the State, to fit out, arm or equip vessels intended to assist in hostile operations against a belligerent, or to supply or conduct such vessels to a belligerent.

It shall be prohibited, within the jurisdiction of the State, to supply arms or ammunition to warships or similar vessels belonging to a belligerent or to assist them to augment their fighting strength.

XIV

It shall be prohibited, within the jurisdiction of the State, to repair warships or similar vessels belonging to a belligerent or to supply them with materials for repairs, tools, supplies, water, or fuel, unless permission has been obtained beforehand from the competent local authorities.

XV

1. It shall be prohibited to form supplies of arms, ammunition, material for repairs, fuel, and any articles useful for the conduct of the war, with the object of seeking an opportunity to hand them over to the maritime forces of a belligerent in close proximity to the territorial sea.

2. Similarly, it shall be prohibited to convey arms, ammunition, material for repairs, fuel or any article useful for the conduct of the war directly out of the territory to belligerent vessels near the coast.

XVI

1. Aircraft shall not be permitted to leave if it is either in a condition to attack a belligerent Power or has on board apparatus or materials the assembling or use of which would enable it to make such attacks, when there is reason to believe that such aircraft is intended to take part in the hostilities.

Similarly, no aircraft shall be permitted to leave if the crew includes any member whatsoever of the fighting forces of a belligerent Power.

It shall be prohibited to execute on an aircraft any work intended to fit it for purposes contrary to the present article.

2. These provisions shall not apply to neutral military aircraft which come within the jurisdiction of the State after the declaration of war, with the permission of the Government.

XVII

It shall be prohibited, within the jurisdiction of the State, to make use of any kind of aircraft whatsoever for aerial observations of the movements, operations, or defence works of a belligerent with the intention of communicating information to the other belligerent.

XVIII

It shall be prohibited, within the jurisdiction of the State, for a belligerent Power or persons in his service to install or operate wireless stations or other means of communication.

XIX

1. It shall be prohibited, within the jurisdiction of the State, to use wireless stations for transmitting information relating to the military forces of the belligerents or to military operations in a belligerent country.

2. Within the jurisdiction of the State, vessels and aircraft may only use their wireless stations for giving signals of distress, for signals essential to navigation, and for transmitting meteorological information.

The Government draws the very serious attention of the population to its duty to comply strictly with the above rules and to avoid any act which would be such as to compromise the neutrality and interests of the country.

Appendix 9

ORDER OF THE DAY OF THE KING TO THE ARMY, SEPTEMBER 4TH, 1939

" TO-DAY I take over the Command of the Army. I do so in the certainty that it will, in all circumstances, show by its valour and self-sacrifice that it is worthy of the confidence which the whole nation places in it."

Appendix 10

SPEECH BY THE KING, BROADCAST TO THE UNITED STATES ON OCTOBER 27TH, 1939

IT is a great honour to me to be speaking from the same platform as your distinguished President. I accepted the Forum's invitation to send a brief message to the American nation with great pleasure.

My fellow-countrymen, my family, and I myself cherish precious and very friendly memories of the United States. Not one Belgian can have forgotten how effectively and sympathetically the American people helped the Belgian people by directing the sending of supplies at a time when we were sorely tried.

I regard the subject proposed—an appeal for the defence of civilization—as a tribute to my country.

Those who suggested it will have had in mind that the Belgians have played a distinguished part in the history of the western world, and that Belgium has always been regarded as one of the centres for the spread of Christian civilization.

I am convinced that my country is defending civilization by the attitude it has adopted towards the European conflict, and so I think I can confine myself to describing it to my American listeners. It is an attitude that is in complete harmony with the desires, the courage, and the honour of my people.

As Head of the State, I am happy to have an opportunity of placing the following facts on record.

In 1937 Belgium proclaimed her independence, and each of her three great neighbours took note of her declaration. Indeed, they went further—they gave us, of their own accord, formal assurances that they would respect our territory and would guarantee the independence of Belgium. The declaration of neutrality by the Belgian Government at the beginning of the war was the logical conclusion of this policy.

Neutrality is, moreover, quite in keeping with the traditions and aspirations of the Belgian people, whose sentiments and attitude of mind were forged during age-long struggles. Belgians, who possess the most acute sense of individual liberty, have paid for their institutions at the cost of their own blood and by their steadfast determination to remain themselves.

Neutrality is also vital to my country's interests. Belgium is a small territory but one of the most densely populated in the world, and she depends mainly for her existence on the labour of her people; and this, in its turn, depends on the maintenance of our export trade and on the free flow of our industrial supplies and our food supplies.

So, for the Belgian people, peace is a matter of life or death.

We have no territorial ambitions whatsoever. Nor have we had anything to do with the origin of the European conflict, either directly or indirectly.

But if Belgium were to become involved in it, her territory would be turned into a battleground; and because her area is so small, that would mean total destruction, whatever might be the outcome of the war.

Belgium, side by side with Holland, stands, in the interests of all, as a peaceful oasis.

Placed at the crossroads of the boundaries of western Europe, Belgium—neutral and loyal—and strong, as she is to-day—fulfils a fundamentally peaceful mission; she sets limits to the battlefield; she wards off family bereavement. Together with the other neutral States she constitutes a citadel of peace; she is a factor making for that spirit of conciliation which alone can save our civilization from the abyss into which general war would precipitate it.

We are quite clear as to our duties and our rights; we await the future calmly and steadfastly, with a clear conscience. We are ready to ensure with all our force that our independence is respected.

Precisely twenty-five years ago to-day, the Belgian Army, after a hard fight, acting under the orders of my father, King Albert, held up a cruel invasion.

Should we be attacked—and may God preserve us from such a fate—in spite of the solemn and categorical undertakings given to us in 1937 and renewed on the eve of the war, we should fight without any hesitation, but with ten times the means; and this time once again the whole country would be behind the Army.

But we cannot believe that the belligerents will fail to respect our neutrality. We have confidence in the promise they made before the whole world, as they in their turn can have confidence in our loyalty. Like my beloved father, I shall always be true to that loyalty, as sovereign of a free and proud nation.

May I venture to hope that the American nation—a nation to whom we feel very near because of our common aspirations and our very similar institutions—will help and sustain us in our efforts to promote the cause of peace in the service of civilization.

Appendix 11

TELEGRAM FROM QUEEN WILHELMINA AND KING LEOPOLD TO THE HEADS OF THE STATES OF GERMANY, FRANCE, AND GREAT BRITAIN, DATED NOVEMBER 7TH, 1939

IN this hour of distress for the whole world, when war, with all its violence, is about to break out in Europe, we feel convinced that it is our duty to speak once again. The belligerent parties declared, a short time ago, that they would be prepared to examine the reasonable and sure bases of an equitable peace. We feel that it would be difficult for them, in the present circumstances, to get into touch with one another in order to explain and reconcile their points of view. We are therefore ready, as sovereigns of two neutral States which are on good terms with all their neighbours, to offer them our good offices. If this should be acceptable to them, we should be prepared by any means in our power which it may please them to suggest to us to facilitate, in a spirit of friendly understanding, enquiry into the factors likely to make for agreement.

That, it seems to us, is the mission we have to fulfil for the good of our peoples and in the interests of the whole world. We hope that our offer will be accepted and that in this way a first step will be made towards the establishment of lasting peace.

(signed) WILHELMINA, LEOPOLD.

THE HAGUE, *November 7th.*

Appendix 12

SPEECH IN THE CHAMBER OF REPRESENTATIVES BY M. SPAAK, MINISTER FOR FOREIGN AFFAIRS, ON DECEMBER 19TH, 1939

M. SPAAK, *Minister for Foreign Affairs and Foreign Trade.*—I should be wanting in gratitude and a sense of justice if, at the beginning of this speech, I did not thank the leaders of groups for the words they have spoken and the sentiments they have expressed.

In the difficult times which are undoubtedly still ahead of us, there could be no more hopeful sign that we shall overcome our difficulties than our unity on foreign policy, a unity from which a people like ours derives its greatest strength.

M. Delwaide, M. Huysmans, and M. Hymans have made my task easy. They have, I feel sure, interpreted the views of the vast majority of the people of this country who approve the Government's foreign policy.

Let it suffice then to repeat here with emphasis that " Belgium is neutral and intends to remain neutral as long as her independence, the integrity of her territory, and her vital interests are not threatened."

In this Belgium is within her rights, and I would add that she is doing her duty to herself.

There is, then, no difference of opinion as to principles. Not one Belgian in a thousand would ask or would desire that we should take part in the war that is rending Europe unless implacable necessity compels us to do so.

That being so, I have no need to explain or justify once more our country's attitude; and I should much prefer to confine myself to emphasizing that public opinion is almost unanimous.

Why then do I offer you explanations ?

Because I feel you ought to know the Government's views on one or two points.

I will enumerate them in the order in which I want to deal with them: (1) Rights and duties of neutrality; (2) Offer of good offices of November 7th and our relations with the Netherlands; (3) Russo-Finnish conflict.

The Government has been accused of taking too narrow, petty and, as it were, pusillanimous a view of neutrality.

 This criticism seems to me to be quite undeserved. The Government is, indeed, very conscious of the difficulties facing it, of its responsibilities. It is undoubtedly in a better position than anyone else to weigh up the dangers we are running and the odds we are up against. It is not surprising, therefore, that its reactions should differ from the reactions of those whose hearts rule their heads. But no one in the Government has ever maintained that neutrality should force us to condone injustice, to remain silent before the cruelties of war. No one has ever maintained that a neutral Belgian must be an indifferent Belgian. And the history of to-day cannot efface the history of yesterday. Such truths have often been proclaimed, and not a member of the Government would deny them. But has not the time come for me to repeat once more—at the risk of boring you—the words of J. Bainville, whose wisdom and profundity I appreciate the more as my experience widens: " You must will the consequences of what you want " ?

The fact that the Belgian State is neutral with the consent—nay more, with the approval—of the vast majority of Belgians, imposes on it certain duties, particularly the duty of loyalty to the belligerents—duties hallowed by tradition. It also entitles the Government to urge that in expressing our views we should cultivate a sense of balance, a sense of proportion and dignity. Quite apart from any legal controversy as to the meaning of neutrality, can you not see that life would soon become impossible, in practice, and that neutrality itself would be singularly compromised, if the neutral State maintained normal relations with all the belligerents, while at the same time its citizens, letting their sense of friendship and their feelings run away with them, lost all sense of proportion and gave free rein to both their sympathies and their antipathies ?

I repeat that to-day personal liberty must be squared with national discipline, and that to sacrifice exaggerated utterances is a very small contribution if it helps to strengthen our position.

I hasten to add that fortunately the situation has greatly improved. The daily Press, in particular, has made a praiseworthy effort, and the moderation with which it supports certain views does not in any way detract—far from it—from their influence.

The almost irreproachable discussions in this Chamber also show that we can be neutral without in any way giving up our intellectual independence; neutral, as we wish to be, without weakness, but also without giving any provocation.

On Tuesday, November 7th, the Queen of the Netherlands and the King of the Belgians again made a united appeal to the belligerents, offering their good offices in seeking " reasonable and sound bases for an equitable peace." Everyone understood, everybody in Belgium approved, the King's action.

M. Carton de Wiart points out in his report that my presence at The Hague was a sure sign that the step taken by our Sovereign was strictly constitutional.

May I say that in the circumstances I am not content with constitutional correctness. I feel I should thank the King in public for the magnificent efforts he has made for several years to spare our country the horrors of war (loud applause); for the wise advice he has always given to the various Governments that came into power one after another; for the strength of mind with which he fulfils his very heavy task; for the example he has always set those with whom he comes into contact, an example which compels respect, admiration, and affection. (Hear, hear.)

Only those who are unwilling to understand can have had any hesitation as to the significance of the appeal of the two Sovereigns and can have attributed to them mysterious motives or aims.

After appealing in very clear terms to the belligerents, offering their good offices, the Queen and King said: This would seem to us to be our mission, a mission we have to fulfil for the good of our own people and in the interests of the whole world.

The good of our people and the interests of the whole world: those two ideals the Sovereigns and their Governments do not dissociate. In seeking to establish reasonable and sound bases for an equitable peace, they intend to devote themselves to this stirring task.

That their words were not heard, that we must assume that it is still too soon and that the hour of peace has not yet struck, I cannot but record with regret, with emotion, with some anxiety, too. And I hope that later on no one will have cause to regret the failure of this effort.

The common effort of the Sovereigns and their Governments provided an opportunity, as the official communiqué of November 7th pointed out, to reaffirm the solidarity of interests of the Netherlands and Belgium.

It has recently been stressed in this Chamber and elsewhere by several speakers; it is sincerely appreciated throughout the whole country.

It is a fact—one of the plainest facts—the most obvious facts—of the present day; and I find it difficult, I must say, to understand why some people close their eyes to it on the misleading pretext that they and they alone defended it here some years ago.

For my part, I have no hesitation in saying that from the military as well as the economic and moral point of view, an independent and neutral Holland is of vital importance to Belgium. I do not think it necessary to labour so obvious a truth.

I am even more anxious than I was—what has happened makes it necessary—that there should be nothing mechanical about

Belgian foreign policy. I want to be quite free to form a judgment in the light of all the facts. For that reason, I think it would be unwise to decide now what attitude we shall have to adopt if the situation in Holland changes. But I should like to make it clear that it would be madness to suppose such an event would leave us indifferent. (Loud applause.)

As far as I am concerned—and I am sure I am speaking for the whole Government—I am deeply conscious of the ties between Belgium and the Netherlands. (Hear, hear.)

The Government is indignant at the Soviet aggression against Finland. (Loud applause from most Parties.)

M. LAHAUT.—Long live the Soviets! (Vehement protests from most benches.) Down with the capitalist war!

THE PRESIDENT.—Order, please, M. Lahaut.

M. RELECOM.—You did not say that, M. Spaak, about Czechoslovakia and Poland! (Lively interruptions from most benches. Uproar.)

M. DELATTRE.—Long live Finland!

M. RELECOM.—Yes, long live the Finnish people!

THE PRESIDENT.—I would ask the Communist members to stop making doubtful comments. (Applause from most benches.)

M. DELATTRE.—Long live the Finnish children, who are being pitilessly massacred! (Several members intervened. The President struck the table with his mallet.)

THE PRESIDENT.—The Minister for Foreign Affairs has the floor and no one else.

M. RELECOM.—The Minister for Foreign Affairs has gone too far.

M. BOHY.—You have gone too far yourself by supporting a foreign Government.

M. LAHAUT.—It is an imperialist war. I am against all imperialism. I am against Italy; I am against Germany. (Violent interruptions.)

THE PRESIDENT.—Order, please, M. Lahaut.

M. LAHAUT.—I don't care. (Loud protests.)

THE PRESIDENT.—Does the Chamber desire it to be recorded in the verbatim report of the meeting that I have just called M. Lahaut to order? (Yes! Yes!)

This proposal was put to the vote and was *adopted* by rising or remaining seated.

M. SPAAK, *Minister for Foreign Affairs and Foreign Trade.*— These interruptions only serve to emphasize that there is unanimity in the Chamber and throughout the country. (Hear, hear.)

We cannot keep silent when an innocent little country is attacked and allow it to be assumed from our silence that we think the attack is justified and even normal.

Even small countries are entitled to live. They too are centres of culture, of civilization, of social progress. And when, like Finland during the past few years, they have carefully avoided diplomatic intrigue, simply affirming their desire to live free and independent among their powerful neighbours, they are entitled to our sympathy in their misfortune. (Loud applause.)

M. SEGHERS (*in Flemish*).—Hear, hear!

M. SPAAK, *Minister for Foreign Affairs and Foreign Trade.*— When, like Finland, they fight one to ten or twenty they also have a right to our admiration. (Hear, hear.)

In its misfortune, the Finnish Government turned to the League of Nations. What could they hope for from this appeal to law when law was daily broken?

Did they still believe in collective security? I doubt it, and I can assure you that I heard of this step with a pang.

Was I wrong? I do not want to judge other people. I know what very complicated and dangerous situations can arise. All I want is to justify Belgium's attitude.

The Soviet Union, a Member of the League of Nations—and what a Member!—attacked Finland, another Member of the League. The Soviet Union refused to attend to explain the matter, and contemptuously—I might almost say cynically— refused every proposal for an understanding, preferring force to any form of conciliation.

The Argentine Republic proposed that the Soviet Union be suspended from the League. I did not feel the Belgian Government could have the slightest hesitation. Consequently it voted in the Council of the League for the suspension of the Soviet Union.

No one asked me for any explanation whatever, for everyone approved. (Hear, hear.)

We know that this gesture had only moral significance. We know that it did not give effective help to Finland.

It is very difficult for little countries, at a distance from one another, to testify to their feeling of fellowship. We are powerless before this tragedy, but we are ready to collaborate in any humanitarian work that may serve, however slightly, to alleviate the sufferings of an heroic people. (Interruptions from the Communists.)

Appendix 13

SECRET INSTRUCTIONS TO THE COMMANDER OF
THE 2ND LUFTFLOTTE FOUND IN A GERMAN
AEROPLANE ON JANUARY 10TH, 1940

THE following documents were in possession of a Staff Major
of the 7th Air Division (parachutist and transport of troops by
air—Headquarters at Berlin) who made a forced landing in
Belgium on January 10th, 1940. The Major had been attached
to Unit 220 of Troop Transport by Air (Fl.F.220), and, when
captured, was flying to Cologne to discuss the scheme at the 22nd
Infantry Division headquarters. Our Intelligence had ascertained
the 22nd Division as specially trained for landing from the air in
enemy territory.

DOCUMENT I

Air Force Command Instructions, 2.....................
File of 17/11/39 to be destroyed (?).......................
pp. the Commander-in-Chief of the Air Force
The Chief of Staff
by order

(signature undecipherable)
Lieutenant-Colonel, General Staff.

	Copy No.
TO:—	
IV Aviation Corps	1
VIII Aviation Corps	2
7 Aviation Division	3
Commander of Air Carrier No. 220 *and to* 22*nd Infantry*	
Division	4
II Anti-Aircraft Defence Corps	5
Headquarters of VI Air Region	6
Headquarters of XI Air Region	7
Reconnaissance Group No. 122	8
For the information of:	
G.H.Q. of Air Force	9
B Group of Armies ..	10
Also to the Air Command ..	11
Liaison Officers at B Group of Armies	12
Army Headquarters, No. 6 ..	13

Air Force Command..   14
Staff:
Staff-Commander   15
Chief of Staff 16
Deputy Chief of Staff   17
Intelligence Section   18
Operations Section, No. 2 19
A.Q. 20
Officer in Charge of Signals   21
Operations Section, No. 1 22
Reserve   ..   .. 23 & 24

British Army here (?).....................................
between Douai and Calais. Behind the whole of this zone
important operative reserves are held deep in Northern France.

The Belgian Army covers the Liège–Antwerp line with its main
force, lighter forces are in position in front on the Meuse–Scheldt
Canal and on the frontier.

Only light forces of the Dutch Army are in position south of
the Waal.

For weather conditions and information about the enemy: see
I c 1 No. 7212/39 Chief of General Staff of 3/11/39.

3. *The German Western Army* directs its attack between the
North Sea and the Moselle, with the strongest possible air-force
support, through the Belgo-Luxemburg region, with the object
of ....
the largest possible groups of the French Army and of its......

The fortress of Liège and..............................
surrounded (?) ....

Further, it is intended, with the help of part of the force (10th
Army Corps reinforced by 1 Cavalry Division), to seize Dutch
territory, with the exception of Festung Holland.

5. *Composition of Army Group B:* see Appendix 2.

6. *Co-operating Forces:*

(*a*) The 3rd Luftflotte attacks, with all the weight of its aircraft,
the French Air Force on the ground, and prevents it from taking
part in land operations.

Later, it prevents the advance of the French Armies moving
north-east from their concentration areas.

The 3rd Luftflotte co-operates also with its Northern Wing
(1st Aviation Corps) with Army Group B.

(*b*) The X Aviation Corps, directly under orders from Air
Force Headquarters, operates in close co-operation with the

naval forces and the F.d., Luft against the enemy naval forces and, in particular, against the British naval forces.

its reserves and . . . .
With regard to home defence against air attack, the chief object is to protect the ground and war industries organizations.

8. *Forces.*—Disposition of the troops and points to be attacked —see Appendix 1.

9. *Reconnaissance.*
(*a*) Air General Headquarters: reconnaissance to the west of the line Le Havre–Orléans–Bourges–Lyon–Geneva.

(*b*) 2nd Luftflottes: reconnaissance by Reconnaissance Group 122 to the north-west and west of the line Western Frisian Isles–Amsterdam–Antwerp–Brussels–Nivelles (islands and towns included).

Task
(*a*) Find out the disposition of the enemy Air Force in Northern France and Belgium.

(*b*) Watch the areas where the British Army is concentrated, detect as quickly as possible any movements from that area towards Belgium in the direction of Brussels–Ghent.

Left boundary. . . . .
Liège–Charleroi–Valenciennes–Amiens–Dieppe.
(these towns included)
(*f*) Crossing of the frontier by reconnaissance planes first on the day A at H plus 5 minutes.

10. *Task of the VIII Aviation Corps:*
On the first day of the attack, the VIII Aviation Corps supports with part of its forces a landing operation of the VII Aviation Division (see special order).

Closely co-operating with the 6th Army (main action to the west of Maastricht), it supports the advance of the land forces attacking the fortified line and the streams of the basin of the Meuse and destroys the Belgian Army to the west of that region. Attacks against towns and villages during the course of these operations are only permitted if it is *absolutely* certain that they are occupied by troops.

Its fighter squadrons have to obtain command of the air over the area of attack of the 6th Army.

7

DOCUMENT 2

APPRECIATION OF THE SITUATION

1. *Terrain.*

On either side of the Meuse a high plateau with heights rising to . . . . m. Very uneven, in places great differences in height, ravines.

Clayey ground, medium heavy to heavy. Only sparsely (?) populated. The operational area of the Division is on the whole thickly wooded.

The Meuse itself constitutes a marked cleft, deeply cut out. Width of river 100 m. Banks rising steeply and mainly wooded. Observation very difficult.

Parachute troops can be dropped everywhere in . . . . the bridges.

Air-borne troops can only be landed at points 15 km. west of the Meuse on the line Vitrival, M. . . ., Posée.

The country is similar in many respects to that of Freuden . . . and troop movements . . . not very mobile will be hindered. On the other hand, it lends itself to defence by groups . . . widely separated.

2. *Landing Grounds.*

Five landing grounds have been reconnoitred. Of these, three are suitable in mild weather (I, III, V), two are suitable only under certain conditions (II, IV). In frosty weather all are suitable. On the whole some........ 30 per cent. bad landing conditions as for " Enterprise " (?).

The whole of the landing troops of the division can be engaged.

Time required : Parachuting and landing of the 1st (?) Division. .... A slight frost gives most favourable conditions ....reducing as much as possible the jump.......... troops.

3. At the cutting of the Meuse, the Division should.......... (objective)..........and keep open............

Road-bridge of Annevoie.

Road bridge Yvoir (here point of main action).

Bridge Dinant–Namur (north-west............)

4. If the country between the Meuse and the French frontier up to..........should not be occupied by enemy troops, the landing would *at first* be unopposed. The landing grounds to the north can, it is true, be shelled by the heavy guns at Namur (15 km.) if they should be discovered.

However, enemy attacks from the fortress of Namur must be expected very soon, and also perhaps from Charleroi, Philippe-ville, and Givet.

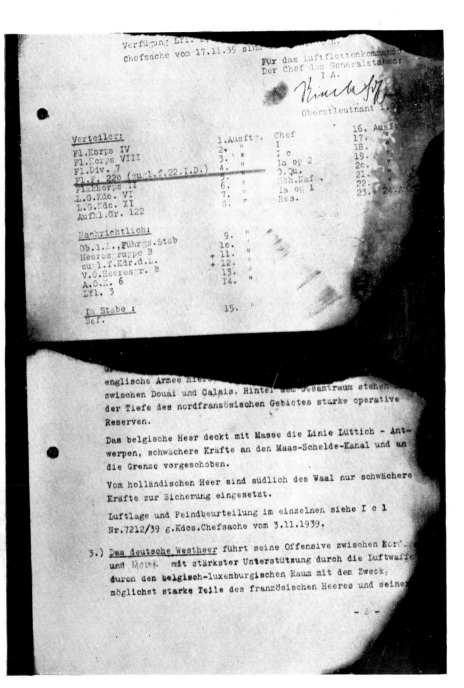

COPY OF SECRET INSTRUCTIONS OF THE GERMAN COMMAND

Straßenbrücke bei Annevoie
Straßenbrücke Yvoir (hier Sch
Bahnbrücke Dinant - Namur (nordwe

4.) Sollte Gebiet zwischen Maas und franz.Grenze bis
feindfrei bleiben, so wird Landung zunächst ungestö
gehen. Nördl. Landeplätze können allerdings durch sch
Flachfeuer von Namur (15 km) gefasst werden, falls sie
frei erkannt werden.

Bald muß jedoch mit feindl. Angriffen aus Fes
Namur, vielleicht auch aus Charleroi, aus Philippeville u
von Givet her gerechnet werden.

Am stärksten bedroht ist die Div. durch schnell
französ.Kräfte aus Linie Maubeuge - Hirson - Fumay (40 km),
deren vorderste Teile nach kürzester Zeit heran sein können.

5.) Daher ist bereits ab Beginn des Landeunternehmens stärkerer
Einsatz eigener Fl.Kampfverbände geboten.

gegen fdl.Versammlungen in Linie Maubeuge - H
- Fumay
gegen Marsch- und Transportbewegungen aus di
Linie
a) auf Straße Mons - Charleroi (besonders
b) auf Straße Maubeuge - Beaumont - Phili
(besonders wichtig),
c) Straße Philippeville - Givet,
d) Straße Fourmies - Chimay - Couvin - G
e) Straße Rocrei - Mariembourg - Philipp
Florennes,
f) Straße Rocroi - Fumay - yet -
Dinant (besonders wic
g) Bahnlinie Mons -
wichtig),
h) Bahnlinie
i) Bahnlin
son

COPY OF SECRET INSTRUCTIONS OF THE GERMAN COMMAND

APPENDIX 13

The chief threat to the division is the arrival of mobile French troops from the line Maubeuge–Hirson–Fumay (40 km.), whose advance units can be on the spot in a very short time.

5. *This is why it is essential that, from the beginning of the landing operation, large forces of our own bomber aircraft should be engaged:*
—against enemy concentrations on the line Maubeuge–Hi
.........Fumay;
—against troops and transport moving from that line:
(a) on the road Mons–Charleroi (especially important);
(b) on the road Maubeuge–Beaumont–Philippeville (specially important);
(c) road Philippeville–Givet;
(d) road Fourmies–Chimay–Couvin–Givet;
(e) road Rocroi–Mariembourg–Philippeville–Florennes;
(f) road Rocroi–Fumay–Givet–towards......Dinant (specially important);
(g) railway Mons-Charleroi..........(important);
(h) railway Maubeuge..........;
(i) railway Charleroi..........(specially important);
(k) railway PQ.............;
(l) railway...........Hastière..........;
(m) Then, for the protection of the Division............
   road Marche–Leignon–Ach.............;
(n) road Ciney–Evrehailles.
The area where bombing by our own aircraft is forbidden is bounded by:
road Rivière–Florette—to a line 4 km. south of the Sambre railway (?) Chatelet through Gerpinnes, Florennes, up to road Philippeville–Dinant (this railway line is outside the forbidden zone) straight (?) line from the level crossing up to Hermeton (this village outside the zone)—the Meuze up to the Anseremme bridge (bridge included in the zone)—line 4 km. east of the Meuse up to Rivière.

6. *Up and down movements of troops can best take place—* south of Liège—at right angles to the frontier towards the Meuse, through Malmédy–Ciney, i.e. by the shortest route in enemy territory.
In the given weather conditions, any détour would only cause inconvenience.
Anti-aircraft defence is insignificant here. On the other hand, very strong opposition from enemy fighters must be expected (chiefly French fighters).
The landing and fighting zone of the Division lies also..........
of many French aerodromes. French and British aviation

groups also stationed more to the west fly, on their way to the front, near..........

The intervention of the Division with more than 600 tons of transport planes and at this spot where the effect will be most felt by the enemy decides the chief point of concentration of enemy aircraft.

The Division is threatened more from the air than from the ground. This is why strong heavy fighter and fighter aircraft formations are necessary:

(a) for the transport, the parachuting and finally the landing (.......... very strong protection);

(b) for supplies;

(c) against enemy air attacks (continuously..........and not only according to special orders).

In this case this protection should be incessant.......... movement and landing. Greater needs in heavy fighters and .... G....

To satisfy this need..........fighting area should only be 110 km. from the frontier (?)..........and should only imply 200 km. flight over enemy territory...........

DOCUMENT 3

..........*Namur* and the immediate vicinity.......... (21 Art.) and light forces Ard..........between Ourthe (here point of main attack) (..........point) and the Meuse..........2 Cavalry Divisions.

At Charleroi 3rd Regiment of Gendarmerie.

French Forces..........are concentrated on the frontier ....ready to march (to the west of the Meuse).......... Army and parts of the 2nd Army with mechanized cavalry and infantry Divisions. Forward elements in the Givet wedge. To the east of the Meuse positions are in the course of construction along the railway line Namur–Assesse–Ciney–Jemelle.

2. *The Meuse* itself is only defended by light forces stationed at the bridges. On the Meuse between Namur and the frontier no permanent fortifications. Special preparations for demolition and blocking are not known here, but are likely.

The region between the Meuse and the French frontier to the west and to the south-west is entirely free from enemy troops.

3. It must be expected that the hostile Walloon population will

wage *guerrilla warfare* (sharp-shooting from the houses and hedges).

4. The possibility of requisitioning (in order to enable the troops to move rapidly and to keep supplied) should only be considered with reservations owing to the sparsely populated nature of the region.

5. *Defence against enemy aircraft in the area of operations of the 7th Air Division (Fl. Div. 7).*

In the operational area Namur–Dinant—and in the neighbouring region no fighters nor anti-aircraft defence have been detected so far.

Anti-aircraft guns..........assumed at Charleroi.

Fighters.

    At St. Hubert—1 squadron of single-seaters, only at intervals.

    Liège   —1 group of single-seaters.

    Nivelles —1 group of single-seaters.

Besides important concentrations of French fighters in Ra
..........Verdun.

....

....

Grandmenil (33 km. west St. Vith) at intervals.

North of Huy, light anti-aircraft guns.

At St. Hubert, heavy anti-aircraft guns at intervals.

    (s) Student.

This copy certified correct.

Puttner (?)
Major, General Staff.

Appendix 14

SPEECH IN THE SENATE BY M. SPAAK, MINISTER FOR FOREIGN AFFAIRS, ON APRIL 16TH, 1940

M. SPAAK, *Minister for Foreign Affairs and Foreign Trade.*—I feel sure the Senate will understand that I should like to make a short statement at the beginning of this debate.

For nearly eight months, Western Europe has been under arms. Millions of men mount guard round our frontiers and challenge one another.

Ten days ago two nations, two friendly nations, were drawn into the turmoil.

We are following Norway's efforts all the more sympathetically, in that she was always a great lover of peace and was loyally neutral. (Hear, hear.) (Applause from all parties.)

She was therefore in much the same position as ourselves. Her sentiments were our sentiments.

This country had enriched our European civilization by its labour, by its social legislation, by the sum of progress it represents; and in many ways we liked to think of it as a model.

Some of us might have had doubts as to its warlike qualities.

What strikes me most in Norway's heroic stand is that love of peace, respect for neutrality, the often-repeated desire to spare one's country the horrors of war do not in any way diminish but rather heighten fierce determination to defend the soil of the Fatherland when it becomes necessary. (Loud applause from all parties.)

To other countries Norway's attitude will be a lesson and an example. This war, which is spreading, this war which is affecting the most innocent, this war which strikes at those who least deserve it, forces us to consider our own position, to consider what we have done—in a word, to take our own bearings.

I, like all of you no doubt, have often thought during the past few months about our foreign policy during the past five years.

Once again the other evening I reread the different diplomatic documents concerning Belgium and the declarations accompanying them.

And once again I arrived at the reassuring conviction that our foreign policy had been perfectly loyal and clear, perfectly correct. (Hear, hear.)

Few countries can have defined their objectives so clearly; confined themselves to promises they could be sure of keeping; enlightened their neighbours as to their intentions. There was not—there is not—any change, any element of surprise. Whatever happens, nobody can say Belgium deceived them. (Further marks of approval.)

On April 29th, 1937, I said in the Chamber:

" What are the principles on which our foreign policy is based?

" I should like to remind you of them once again. We want first and foremost to find a formula for uniting our people. We do not want to make sacrifices for the sake of a specifically Walloon or specifically Flemish ideology. We want a policy that is solely and exclusively Belgian. We want a policy firmly rooted in our national traditions, a policy which will help us to play our part in Europe.

" Belgium has no direct interests outside her own frontiers; she has no ambition other than to remain what she is; she seeks nothing; she asks nothing of anyone but peace.

" But—and this is both her misfortune and her greatness—she has for centuries been a European batttlefield, a highway for invasion for all the conquerors. Her rôle, the rôle entrusted to her, one she must fulfil, is to close up on all sides and in all directions the way of invasion; to erect so many barriers and create so many difficulties on the battlefield of Europe that even the boldest are deterred.

"That is why our military policy is so closely bound up with our foreign policy. If Europe has more confidence in us to-day, it is not only because of our loyal attitude. It is because a few months ago, for the first time in our history, we all together shouldered the heavy burdens demanded of us."

Two years later, on June 8th, 1939, M. Pierlot in his turn summarized our chief aspirations:

"The main object of our policy of independence, in so far as it rests with us, is to preserve our country from the scourge of war. Belgium is a resolutely pacific country. She is determined not to take up arms except against an aggression directly aimed at her vital interests. In other words, the only ground for war that we would accept is national defence. But in such a case, we are ready to make every sacrifice, because more important than peace are liberty and honour." (Loud cheers.)

These few sentences of which you have just signified your approval, these principles which you have ratified by your votes, still hold good to-day.

In 1935 the Treaty of Locarno was torn up and the last illusion about the League of Nations was shattered. We were faced with this dilemma: an alliance with the Great Powers or independence.

We did not want an alliance, whatever our sympathy with our possible partners, for it would have made of us mediocre followers, it would have involved us in an international policy that we were not strong enough to apply; it would have led us irresistibly to war.

We wanted to remain ourselves, to remain, as far as possible, masters of our fate. We wanted in so doing to play the part which geography and history have assigned to us in Western Europe. We dreamed of being a crossroads where all the great currents of civilization might peacefully cross one another. We have told everybody what we should like to be, what we want to do. It is a good thing, it is useful, to recall to-day that France, Great Britain, and Germany solemnly proclaimed that this policy was justified.

Our neighbours who, at the beginning of the present conflict, solemnly confirmed their determination to respect our territory, have themselves summed up in terms we cannot but accept certain principles underlying our policy.

They have taken note of our determination expressed publicly and on more than one occasion to defend the frontiers of Belgium with all our forces against any aggression or invasion, and to prevent Belgium from being used, for purposes of aggression against another State, as a passage or as a base of operations by land, by sea, or in the air.

Though we have concluded no treaty, in the actual meaning of the word, with France, Great Britain, or Germany, we have entered into a moral undertaking to which we intend to adhere, so long as the situation in Western Europe remains what it is to-day.

International law, international morality, have sustained violent blows in recent times. In spite of all, they remain a refuge for small nations, and, whatever the transgressions of others, Belgium would never be justified in breaking her word.

We shall never give up our chief claim to consideration—our loyalty.

The discreet policy we have adopted is justified by our general desire to avoid war, but also by our more definite desire to avoid becoming once more the battlefield of Europe.

Those in other countries who judge us severely or give us advice, those at home—happily they become fewer every day—who disapprove of the Government's policy, have not understood what will happen to us if this policy fails.

As early as October 14th, 1936, the King said: " In the absence of a defence system of her own, capable of withstanding the invader, the invasion would penetrate deeply into Belgium at the very beginning and she would be devastated at once. Afterwards friendly intervention might, of course, ensure final victory, but in the process the country would suffer ravages such as would be infinitely worse than those of the war of 1914–18."

No country wants war; no country would agree to be a field of battle.

The Scandinavian countries showed this during the Finnish war. The Balkan countries are wise and sensible, and do not risk lighting a fire that would, they realize, assume devastating proportions.

The great belligerent countries themselves have taken their precautions.

France has her Maginot line; Germany has her Siegfried line; Great Britain has the sea.

Behind this triple belt, they can face the idea of war because they feel safe. Belgium could not build ramparts on her threatened frontiers: it would have been out of proportion to her resources. She did what she could in the military sphere, and she is happy to have done so, but she sought rather to complement her security in the diplomatic field.

I do not want to paint a picture of the horrors our country might have to endure if it were involved in war—it would be only too easy to do so.   But I venture to say that our fate would be worse than that of any other belligerent.   This alone is sufficient justification for our efforts, and I am not ashamed of egoism, the sacred egoism which inspires me when I am fighting to spare Belgium an ordeal she has not deserved.   (Loud applause.)

All these ideas, all these principles, were ours before the war. We have been guided by them for the past eight months, and we still believe in them.

I am glad to say we have not had a single incident with the belligerents that has led to a really serious situation.

Twice only—at Nivelles at the beginning of the war and, more tragically, at St. Hubert a few weeks ago—we have had to deplore some injured and one dead.   Each time our rights were fully recognized; each time we were compensated for the damage done.

In a very difficult situation, placed as we are between great neighbours engaged in a formidable struggle, we stood firm without flinching.   There was, I swear, no provocation, no boasting; nor was there any lack of firmness and dignity.

What helps us, what has saved us so far—I shall never weary of repeating—is our loyalty.   Here, as in the economic and military spheres, we have done everything we could and everything we should.

We have brought the country's fighting strength up to the highest pitch, and we have never lost sight of the fact that at present we must depend first and foremost on ourselves.

The public is anxious, and I can quite understand that.   Their anxiety makes them too ready to listen to certain rumours.   We must, by displaying calm, help them to overcome this tendency. Belgians can be sure that the Government will not accept any suggestion calculated to change our policy, a policy approved by the vast majority of the people.

We have a very difficult task ahead of us; our responsibilities are very heavy.   The whole future of Belgium is at stake.   We are therefore entitled to ask for your confidence and your help.

We are also entitled to ask you to show that national discipline which is so necessary to-day.   We in the Government have sympathies and friendships too, but far above friendship is duty. Love of friendship is very precious, and we all would willingly give ourselves up to it.   The path of duty is rougher; yet we must choose it.

Above all, we must protect our people; we must spare them

war; we must save our children; we must safeguard our towns and our countryside.

Our duty as leaders—our duty as men—is above all to preserve peace.

It is also our duty, should our independence or our vita interests be threatened, to be strong enough effectively to defend them.

The country desires peace; the country desires neutrality. The country will do its duty all the better if it is compelled to do so, if it has the deep conviction, the absolute assurance, that its leaders have done their utmost to preserve peace and neutrality.

That is our duty—our difficult but splendid duty.

If you are only willing to help us, we shall succeed. (Loud applause, except from the Communists.)

Appendix 15

NOTE BY THE MINISTRY OF NATIONAL DEFENCE, DATED MARCH 28TH, 1940, ON THE DEFENSIVE WORKS CARRIED OUT SINCE THE BEGINNING OF THE CONFLICT

A FORMIDABLE steel barrier divides the interior of the country and forms a practically impassable barrier to probable attacks by armoured tanks. The wall of steel constructed by our untrained builders is at present 70 km. long. It represents a weight of over 30,000 tons; 34,000 tons of steel framework, 1,000 tons of steel cables, 150 tons of camouflage colouring, and about 600 tons of various materials. Thus, 35,000 tons of steel have been put in position in open country, across fields, woods and marshes, floods, rivers and railways, leaving no loophole for the assailant.

Every difficulty has been overcome—gradients, mud, water. Neither rain nor snow nor cold have stopped the work for one second. In temperatures as low as − 16°, when the cold was so intense that the heavy pieces of steel stuck to the hands of the men, they doggedly continued to raise this formidable barrier across our fields and woods. From November 1st to December 31st, during the rainiest season, when the winter was already very severe, our soldiers raised a steel wall 30 km. long in a sea of mud, in water and in the cold.

Appendix 16

MEASURES TAKEN BY BELGIUM TO STRENGTHEN THE NATIONAL DEFENCE SYSTEM

THE object of these measures is:
1. To reinforce the fortified system and to strengthen the protective measures of the country.
2. To increase the number of effectives on a war footing.
3. To modernize and augment material and armament.

I. THE BELGIAN FORTIFIED SYSTEM AND PROTECTIVE MEASURES

The construction of the Belgian fortified system, which was begun in 1928, was continued at an ever-increasing speed down to May 1940. The plan for the fortified system and protective measures was closely connected with the plan of campaign, and the two were developed on parallel lines.

In the Province of Liège

The rearming and modernization of eight old forts at Liège (the six forts on the right bank and the forts of Flemalle and Pontisse on the left bank) was begun in 1928.

To meet the danger of a sudden attack, designed to hamper the mobilization of the Belgian Army, a chain of pillboxes against invasion was established on the line running from Jupille, Chenée, and Renory, covering all the roads into Liège. They were equipped with 47-mm. guns, searchlights, machine-guns, and sub-machine guns, and were guarded by anti-tank obstacles. They were manned permanently. For the same purpose, fortified posts covering important road junctions were constructed near the frontier at Homburg, Henrichapelle, Dolhain, Jalhaye, and Malmedy.

In the gaps between the old forts, a beginning was made in 1934 with the construction of flanking casemates for automatic weapons.

After these measures of security had been taken, the construction was begun of a new fortified line comprising the new forts of Eben-Emael, Neufchateau, Battice, and Pepinster, and a number of flanking casemates for automatic weapons were constructed in the gaps between these works.

From the frontier to the Meuse there were several lines along which provision had been made for the destruction of roads and bridges, the efficacy of which depended on fire from the new and old forts.

The fortified town was also provided with an underground telephone system, control-rooms, a planned road system, gun-emplacements for heavy artillery on railway-tracks, stores of ammunition and materials. To guard, maintain, and man all these fortifications and to carry out demolition work it was necessary to form special units on a voluntary basis. These consisted of battalions of cyclist frontier guards.

In the Provinces of Limburg and Antwerp

The defences had necessarily to follow the water-lines. Defensive structures were established, in the first place, along the canal from Maastricht to Bois-le-Duc and the canal joining the Meuse and the Escaut. They consisted of:

Casemates for automatic weapons enfilading the water-level and pillboxes covering the bridges;

Arrangements for flooding and demolition work.

As the *Albert Canal* was cut, similar works were constructed. They were finished in 1939.

The Limburg structures, when completed, were linked up with the fortified town of Liège by the Eben-Emael fort.

In the Provinces of Namur and Luxemburg

The defence system was based on the fortified town of Namur, which was rearmed and modernized on the same lines as the fortified town of Liège (ring of old forts; pillboxes in the gaps, line of pillboxes against invasion, fortified posts on the frontier, progressive lines of demolition). In order to take advantage of the broken Ardennes country, a division of "Chasseurs Ardennais," specially trained in skirmishing, was formed. Tactics of this kind, which would be facilitated by the valleys and by demolition work, were calculated to inflict heavy losses on an invader and to cause considerable delay.

From 1936 *onward*, the Government was obliged, because of the repudiation by Germany of the military clauses of the Treaty of Versailles and the Treaty of Locarno, to strengthen the national defence system still further. Its aim was to build up a military machine sufficiently strong to discourage Belgium's neighbours from attempting to use Belgium as a battlefield or as a base for an attack. From the military standpoint, the risks involved by the changed situation in Europe had two consequences:

1. *It became necessary to strengthen the protective measures.*

The period of military service was extended to a year, and a considerable part of the contingent in the 1937–41 classes was required to do seventeen months' service.

2. *It became necessary to modify the fortified system.*

The concrete and iron framework established on the frontier on the Antwerp–Liège–Namur line could no longer be used as the backbone for a position of resistance. The Belgian Army could not hold a front over 200 km. long.

In 1939, the construction of a fortified position on the Antwerp–Namur line was begun. This position, known as K.W. from the names of the terminal points (Koningshoyckt and Wavre), consisted of a number of works disposed on several lines. They were protected in front by a continuous anti-tank barricade and by flooding, whilst anti-tank traps were set deep in the position. An underground telephone system and a planned road system completed the equipment of the position. These works were completed in May 1940.

II. INCREASE IN THE NUMBER OF EFFECTIVES ON A WAR FOOTING

In 1930 the Belgian Army had one cavalry corps consisting of two divisions and three army corps each consisting of two divisions of infantry on a war footing. It was obvious that its military machine was inadequate. Six reserve divisions (with the same composition as the divisions on active service) were therefore put into working order. In 1936 it was decided to organize six divisions of the second reserve. For protective purposes, a division of " Chasseurs Ardennais " was formed.

In August 1939, the Belgian Army had on a war footing:
1 cavalry corps consisting of 2 cavalry divisions and a brigade of motorized cavalry;
5 army corps and 2 reserve army corps, consisting in all of:
12 divisions on active service and in the reserve;
2 divisions of " Chasseurs Ardennais ";
6 divisions of the second reserve;
1 brigade of cyclist frontier guards.
On May 10th, 1940, the Belgian Army consisted of 650,000 regulars.

It was the strongest Army Belgium had ever had. The order for general mobilization brought the strength up to over 900,000 men, representing more than one-tenth of the population—that is to say, the maximum military effort of which a country is capable.

III. MODERNIZATION AND AUGMENTATION OF ARMS

A small, peaceful country must organize, train, and equip its Army for the defensive.

Acting on this principle, the Belgian General Staff rejected *a priori* the idea of forming a military air force and armoured units and devoted the maximum credits to acquiring defensive weapons.

The *infantry* was well-equipped with a very valuable anti-tank arm: the 47-mm. gun (sixty 47-mm. guns to each infantry division). It was provided with new bomb-throwers; its sub-machine-guns were renewed, the rifles being brought up to date, and the number of 75-mm. mortars was trebled.

The *artillery* was expanded. Provision was made for increasing the number of groups in the infantry divisions from four to five and those in the Army Corps from four to six. As an experiment, part of the artillery of the Army Corps was motorized. A new Land Anti-Aircraft Defence Gun (40-mm. Bofors gun) was put into service.

The *light troops* were completely motorized. Their mobility and radius of action were thus very considerably enlarged.

Lastly, having regard to the primary importance of communications in modern warfare, the Belgian Army was equipped with a considerable amount of first-rate telephone and wireless material.

That, in broad outline, is a description of the military burden which Belgium took upon herself. No sacrifice in either men or money was spared. The number of army effectives on a war footing was over 10 per cent. of the population, a figure which was not reached by the belligerent nations during the 1914–18 War. The expenditure incurred in setting up a military machine of this magnitude and in constructing our fortified system increased year by year, and in 1939 it amounted to 20 per cent. of the total budget.

Appendix 17

TEXT OF THE PROTEST COMMUNICATED BY THE BELGIAN GOVERNMENT TO THE FOREIGN GOVERNMENTS FOLLOWING UPON THE GERMAN AGGRESSION OF MAY 10TH, 1940

ALTHOUGH Germany has not declared war, the German Army has just crossed the frontier of the Kingdom of Belgium and has attacked the Belgian Army with considerable forces. All the facts and all the documents in the possession of the Belgian Government prove that the aggression was premeditated. No complaint was brought to its notice before the act of aggression. Moreover, there was nothing in the relations between the two countries, for the most part good, to suggest that a conflict was likely to arise. The Belgian Government protests against this outrage. It points out that for the second time in twenty-five years Belgium has been the victim of an aggression by Germany. In its declaration of October 13th, 1937, the German Government solemnly confirmed its determination in no circumstances to impair the inviolability and integrity of Belgium and stated that " it will at all times respect Belgian territory, except, of course, in the event of Belgium's taking part in a military action directed against Germany in an armed conflict in which Germany is involved," declaring that it was prepared to assist Belgium should she be subjected to an attack or to invasion. On August 26th, in a spontaneous declaration, the German Government solemnly renewed its undertaking of October 13th, 1937. Since making the Declaration in 1937, Germany has on many occasions paid tribute to the correctness of the attitude maintained by Belgium. Public opinion is unanimous in recognizing that the Belgian Government has done everything in its power to avert the scourge of war which threatened Europe. On the eve of the European War, the King of the Belgians, in conjunction with the Heads of other States, and more particularly with Her Majesty the Queen of the Netherlands, took steps to avert the danger. It is sufficient to recall the appeal made from Brussels on August 23rd, 1939, on behalf of the Heads of the States of the Oslo Group and the offer of good offices on the 29th of the same month. A further offer of good offices was made on November 7th by the Queen of the Netherlands and the King of the Belgians, with a view to facilitating enquiry into points on which agreement could be reached. During the conflict, Belgium has always observed strict and scrupulous neutrality. She was attacked suddenly at dawn. The aggression was consummated when the Government appealed to the guarantor Powers. Just as in August 1914, Germany violated Belgian neutrality which she had guaranteed in virtue of the treaties of April 19th, 1839, so to-day she has attacked Belgium in contravention of an undertaking contracted in 1937 and renewed in 1939, the validity of which is not open to question. As in 1914, an act of aggression against a neutral State, while not justified in itself, is made worse by the violation of undertakings that had been entered into. This new outrage will deeply shock the conscience of the world. The German Reich will be held responsible by history for the sufferings which this act of aggression will inflict on the Belgian people. Belgium has never accepted servitude. She will suffer her ordeal courageously. The Belgian Army will defend Belgian national territory with all its force, with the help of Belgium's guarantors, who will not fail to fulfil their promises.

Appendix 18

PROCLAMATION BY KING LEOPOLD, MAY 10TH, 1940

BELGIANS, for the second time in a quarter of a century, Belgium —a loyal and neutral country—has been attacked by the German Empire in spite of the most solemn undertakings contracted before the whole world. The Belgian people, who are fundamentally peaceful, have done everything in their power to prevent this, but between sacrifice and dishonour the Belgian of 1940 will hesitate no more than did the Belgian of 1914.

By awaiting the actual violation of our territory before appealing to our two guarantors, who have remained faithful to their promises, we have most loyally fulfilled to the last the duties of neutrality.

To our valiant Army, to our courageous soldiers, I address the greetings of the country. In them we place complete confidence. Worthy successors of the heroes of 1914, they will fight shoulder to shoulder to stop the onrush of the enemy through our provinces and to restrict the area of our national territory which is violated by the invader.

Thanks to the efforts which our country agreed to make, our fighting forces are infinitely more powerful than they were in 1914.

France and Great Britain have promised to help us. Their advance troops are already pushing forward to join up with ours. The fight will be hard. Great sacrifices and deprivation will be asked of you. But there can be no doubt about the final victory. I intend to remain faithful to my constitutional oath to maintain the independence and integrity of the territory. Like my father in 1914, I have put myself at the head of the Army with the same faith, the same clear conscience. The cause of Belgium is pure. With the help of God it will triumph.

Appendix 19

TRANSLATION OF TEXT BELOW MAP

COMRADES !

HERE is the situation !
In any case, the war is over for you !
Your leaders are going to escape by airplane.
Lay down your arms !

Camarades!

Telle est la situation!
En tout cas, la guerre est finie pour vous!
    Vos chefs vont s'enfuir par avion.
A bas les armes!

British Soldiers!

Look at this map: it gives your true situation!
Your troops are entirely surrounded —
    stop fighting!
Put down your arms!

COPY OF GERMAN LEAFLETS DROPPED IN THE BELGIAN LINES

Appendix 20

KING LEOPOLD'S ORDER OF THE DAY, MAY 25TH, 1940

Translation of Text in Flemish and French

SOLDIERS:

THE great battle which we were expecting has commenced.

It will be hard. We will carry it on with all our strength and with supreme energy.

It is being fought on the ground where in 1914 we stood victoriously against the invader.

SOLDIERS:

Belgium expects that you will do honour to her Flag.

OFFICERS AND MEN:

Whatever happens, my fate will be yours.
I ask of you all firmness, discipline, trust.
Our cause is just and pure.
Providence will help us.
LONG LIVE BELGIUM!

LEOPOLD.

In the field, the 25th of May, 1940.

Appendix 21

STATEMENT BY LIEUT.-COL. ROBERT DUNCAN BROWN, UNITED STATES MILITARY ATTACHÉ TO BELGIUM AND LUXEMBURG

THE German Armies in May 1940, supported by immense Air Power, drove west into Holland, Belgium, and France, quickly conquered Holland and broke the hinge of Allied Defence at Sedan. The Sedan break-through compelled the retreat of all Northern Allied forces and separated the British and Belgian Forces from the French Main Forces. A French counter-attack against the German spear-head aimed at Abbeville might have re-established the situation but this counter-attack never developed.

The Belgian Army fought doggedly on successive retreat positions and at last found themselves completely cut off with their backs to the sea. Their artillery had fought with extreme

Soldaten,

De groote slag die ons te wachten staat, is begonnen.

Hij zal hard zijn. Wij zullen hem voeren, met al onze krachten en met een uiterste inspanning.

Deze slag wordt geleverd op het grondgebied, waar we in 1914 aan den overweldiger zegevierend weerstand geboden hebben.

Soldaten,

België verwacht van U, dat gij Uw Vaandel eer zult aandoen.

Officieren, Soldaten,

Wat er ook moge gebeuren, mijn lot zal het Uwe zijn.

Ik vraag aan allen vastberadenheid, tucht en vertrouwen. Onze zaak is rechtvaardig en rein.

De Voorzienigheid zal ons helpen.

Leve België !

LEOPOLD.

Te velde, den 25 Mei 1940.

Soldats,

La grande bataille qui nous attendait a commencé.

Elle sera rude. Nous la conduirons de toutes nos forces avec une suprême énergie.

Elle se livre sur le terrain où en 1914 nous avons tenu victorieusement tête à l'envahisseur.

Soldats,

La Belgique attend que vous fasulez honneur à son Drapeau.

Officiers, Soldats,

Quel qu'il arrive, mon sort sera le vôtre.

Je demande à tous de la fermeté, de la discipline, de la confiance.

Notre cause est juste et pure.

La Providence nous aidera.

Vive la Belgique !

LEOPOLD.

En campagne, le 25 mai 1940.

THE KING'S ORDER OF THE DAY TO THE ARMY, MAY 25TH, 1940

brilliancy, their large units were well led. However, they were cut off and they had virtually no air power or anti-aircraft artillery protection against German air might.

The Belgian King's capitulation on May 28th was the only thing that King Leopold could do. Those who say otherwise didn't see the fighting and they didn't see the German Air Force. I saw both.

ROBERT DUNCAN BROWN.

October 31st, 1940.

Appendix 22
HIGH COURT OF JUSTICE
June 13th, 1941
KING'S BENCH DIVISION

Sir Roger Keyes *v.* Daily Mirror Newspapers Limited
Before Mr. Justice Tucker

Sir Patrick Hastings, K.C., and Mr. Valentine Holmes appear for Sir Roger Keyes ; Mr. G. O. Slade for the defendants.

Statement made by Sir Patrick Hastings:
This is an action for libel brought by Admiral of the Fleet Sir Roger Keyes against the Daily Mirror Newspapers Limited in consequence of an article which appeared in the *Daily Mirror* newspaper of May 30th, 1940.

The Germans invaded Belgium on May 10th, and a few hours later Sir Roger Keyes, at the request of our Government, left England by aeroplane to join King Leopold as special liaison officer. He was with the King at the Headquarters of his Army throughout the brief campaign in Belgium, and at the same time was in close touch with the Headquarters of the British Army and with the Government. He remained with King Leopold until 10 p.m. on the night of May 27th, the day on which King Leopold asked the Germans for an armistice. During that time he had unrivalled opportunities of observing the course of events.

On May 28th, Mr. Churchill announced in the House of Commons that the surrender had taken place and asked that judgment about the matter should be suspended until the facts were known.

Sir Roger Keyes on the same day, in the lobby, echoed the same advice and trusted that judgment on King Leopold, a very gallant soldier, should be suspended till all the facts became known.

This advice did not appeal to the persons responsible for the conduct of the *Daily Mirror* newspaper, and on May 30th that paper published a diatribe attacking violently not only the King of the Belgians but also Sir Roger Keyes.

How far justified Sir Roger was in his advice to suspend judgment is now beginning to be understood.

King Leopold, when his country was invaded, had placed himself and his Army under the French High Command, and the movements of his Army conformed with the orders of the French Command.

On May 20th, the British Army and French Northern Army were ordered to prepare to fight to the south-westward to regain contact with the main French Army, and unless the Belgian Army could conform to this movement it was clear that it would involve a breach of contact between the British and Belgian Armies.

Sir Roger informed the King of the order, and he was asked by the King to inform the British Government and Lord Gort that the Belgian Army had neither tanks nor aircraft and existed solely for defence. He did not feel he had any right to expect the British Government to jeopardize, perhaps, the very existence of the British Army in order to keep contact with the Belgian Army, but he wished to make it quite clear that if there were a separation between the two Armies, the capitulation of the Belgian Army would be inevitable.

At the request of the French High Command the Belgian Army was withdrawn on May 23rd from the strongly prepared position on the Scheldt to a much weaker and longer line on the Lys, to allow the British Army to retire behind the defensive frontier line which it had occupied throughout the winter, in order to prepare for the offensive it was about to undertake to the southward.

On the evening of May 26th, a break through the Belgian line by the Germans seemed to be inevitable and the King moved the remaining French 60th Division in Belgian vehicles to a prepared position across the Yser, which by now was flooded over a wide area and its bridges mined.

Fighting on the Belgian front had been continuous for four days, and the Belgian Army, by May 27th, was running short of food and ammunition and was being attacked by at least eight German divisions, including armoured units and wave after wave of dive bombers.

On the morning of May 27th, the King asked Sir Roger to

inform the British authorities that he would be obliged to surrender before a debacle took place. A similar message was given to the French.

By the afternoon of that day the German Army had driven a wedge between the Belgian and British Armies. Every road, village, and town in the small part of Belgium left in Belgian hands was thronged with hundreds of thousands of refugees, and men, women, and children were being mercilessly bombed and machine-gunned by low-flying aircraft.

In these circumstances, at 5 p.m. on the 27th, King Leopold informed the British and French authorities that he intended at midnight of that day to ask for an armistice so as to avoid further slaughter of his people.

This message, like the earlier one on the same day, was promptly received in London and Paris, but all communications with the British Army were cut, and though wireless messages were repeatedly made, it is now known that these did not reach the Commanders-in-Chief.

Sir Roger Keyes, knowing these facts as he did, with a number of details that are unnecessary for the purposes of this statement, felt more than justified in suggesting a suspension of judgment on the King, and he quite naturally resented the insult and injury of the article in the *Daily Mirror* attacking him. He immediately saw his solicitors and the present action was started.

The defence to the action pleaded that the words of the libel, so far as they were statements of fact were true in substance and in fact, and so far as they were expressions of opinion that they were fair comment.

Wiser counsel subsequently prevailed, and this defence was withdrawn by a letter from the Defendants' Solicitors in the following words :

Temple Chambers,
Temple Avenue, E.C.4.
October 9th, 1940.

DEAR SIRS,

KEYES *v.* DAILY MIRROR

Our Clients have been advised by Counsel that as a matter of law their defence of fair comment in this action cannot succeed unless they can substantiate the statements of fact in the article complained of with reference to the conduct of King Leopold.

Our Clients are not in a position to prove these statements to be true and we should accordingly be glad if you would treat this letter as a formal notice that their plea of fair comment will no longer be relied upon.

Whether the strictures passed upon King Leopold by, amongst others, the Prime Minister of France, were in fact justified, our Clients have no means of knowing; all they can say is that if there was the slightest doubt about the matter, nothing could have been more dignified and proper than your Client's request for a suspension of judgment upon King Leopold and nothing more creditable than that your Client should have made the request at the time that he did, when everyone's hand was against the King.

As the whole criticism of your Client in the article complained of was based upon facts which our Clients then believed and had the highest possible authority for believing to be true, but which they must now assume to be untrue, it follows that every vestige of foundation for such criticism disappears, and our Clients are accordingly desirous of making honourable amends to your Client, who has acted throughout in accordance with the highest traditions of honour and justice.

Our Clients invite your Client to say what he would like them to do as an earnest of their sincerity in making this offer, since they feel that he will not want to fasten too much responsibility upon them for acting upon information coming from sources which they had every right to regard as unimpeachable.

Upon this last aspect of the case our Clients will be serving a notice in mitigation of damages if it should still be necessary for this action to proceed to trial.

Yours faithfully,
SHIRLEY WOOLMER & Co.

Messrs. Alfred Cox & Son,
37, Norfolk Street,
Strand, W.C.2.

After this withdrawal and the acceptance and publication of the foregoing statement, there was nothing left of the action except the question of damages, and these have now been agreed.

The further account of the proceedings was given by *The Times* of June 14th, 1941, as follows :

Mr. Slade said that his Lordship would observe from the papers before him how unimpeachable had been the defendants' sources of information as to the conduct ascribed to the King of the Belgians in seeking an armistice from the Germans on May 27th, 1940. The defendants accepted without reservation the statement just made by Sir Patrick Hastings, from which it would appear that they had been entirely misled. They welcomed the opportunity of repeating in open Court the sentiments expressed in their solicitors' letter of October 9th, 1940.

Sir Roger Keyes's dignified and fair-minded attitude towards the King of the Belgians had been abundantly justified, and the defendants tendered to the gallant Admiral a sincere apology for their criticism of him, coupled with an expression of their appreciation of his conduct and bearing throughout.

The matter did not, however, end there. It was apparent from the facts stated on behalf of Sir Roger Keyes that a very grave injustice had been done to the King of the Belgians, who, like Sir Roger Keyes, had acted throughout in accordance with the highest traditions of honour and justice. The defendants accordingly wished to take advantage of the opportunity to tender also to King Leopold, who was not now in a position to defend himself, their most sincere and respectful apology for the injustice which they had unwittingly done him. They hoped that if and when their apology came to the knowledge of King Leopold he would accept it in the spirit in which it was offered.

Mr. Justice Tucker, in assenting to the settlement and to the withdrawal of the record, said that this libel action, unlike some others, appeared to have served a most useful purpose, and the statements which had been made would give very wide satisfaction.

Solicitors:—Messrs. Alfred Cox & Son; Messrs. Shirley Woolmer & Co.

Made and Printed in Great Britain by
Hazell, Watson & Viney, Ltd.
London and Aylesbury.

INVENTORY '80